THE HOLLYWOOD
FILM MUSICAL

NEW APPROACHES TO FILM GENRE

Series Editor: Barry Keith Grant

New Approaches to Film Genre provides students and teachers with original, insightful, and entertaining overviews of major film genres. Each book in the series gives an historical appreciation of its topic, from its origins to the present day, and identifies and discusses the important films, directors, trends, and cycles. Authors articulate their own critical perspective, placing the genre's development in relevant social, historical, and cultural contexts. For students, scholars, and film buffs alike, these represent the most concise and illuminating texts on the study of film genre.

From Shane *to* Kill Bill: *Rethinking the Western*, Patrick McGee
The Horror Film, Rick Worland
Hollywood and History, Robert Burgoyne
The Religious Film, Pamela Grace
The Hollywood War Film, Robert Eberwein
The Fantasy Film, Katherine A. Fowkes
The Multi-Protagonist Film, María del Mar Azcona
The Hollywood Romantic Comedy, Leger Grindon
Film Noir, William Luhr
The Hollywood Film Musical, Barry Keith Grant

THE HOLLYWOOD
FILM MUSICAL

Barry Keith Grant

(J)WILEY-BLACKWELL

A John Wiley & Sons, Ltd., Publication

This edition first published 2012
© 2012 Barry Keith Grant

Blackwell Publishing was acquired by John Wiley & Sons in February 2007. Blackwell's
publishing program has been merged with Wiley's global Scientific, Technical, and Medical
business to form Wiley-Blackwell.

Registered Office
John Wiley & Sons Ltd, The Atrium, Southern Gate, Chichester, West Sussex, PO19 8SQ, UK

Editorial Offices
350 Main Street, Malden, MA 02148-5020, USA
9600 Garsington Road, Oxford, OX4 2DQ, UK
The Atrium, Southern Gate, Chichester, West Sussex, PO19 8SQ, UK

For details of our global editorial offices, for customer services, and for information
about how to apply for permission to reuse the copyright material in this book please
see our website at www.wiley.com/wiley-blackwell.

The right of Barry Keith Grant to be identified as the author of this work has been
asserted in accordance with the UK Copyright, Designs and Patents Act 1988.

Library of Congress Cataloging-in-Publication Data

Grant, Barry Keith, 1947-
The Hollywood Film Musical / Barry Keith Grant.
       p. cm. – (New approaches to film genre)
  Includes bibliographical references and index.
  ISBN 978-1-4051-8253-9 (hardcover : alk. paper) – ISBN 978-1-4051-8252-2 (pbk. : alk. paper)
  1. Musical films–United States–History and criticism. I. Title.
  PN1995.9.M86G68 2012
  791.43'6578–dc23

                                                                                       2011044943

A catalogue record for this book is available from the British Library.

Set in 11/13pt, Bembo by Thomson Digital, Noida, India
Printed in Malaysia by Ho Printing (M) Sdn Bhd

1   2012

For Rob and Terrance,
friends who step to the music they hear,
both far away and near

CONTENTS

LIST OF PLATES

All illustrations are from the author's personal collection except as indicated.

ACKNOWLEDGMENTS

This book would not have come to be without the wisdom and patience of Jayne Fargnoli, Executive Editor at Wiley-Blackwell. She is the ideal editor whom authors dream about. Galen Smith, Margot Morse, Allison Kostka, and Lisa Eaton at Wiley-Blackwell have been a pleasure to work with. Justin Dyer copy-edited the manuscript with the careful and detailed attention that it deserved. I am also grateful to David Desser for his careful and appreciative reading of the manuscript, and his helpful suggestions for revision.

And, as always, my wife Genevieve Habib has provided magnificent support in so many ways while I was writing.

INTRODUCTION

While definition of the film musical is a matter of some debate, we might say that as a distinct genre, the musical refers to films that involve the performance of song and/or dance by the main characters and also include singing and/or dancing as an important element. Movies that feature an occasional musical interlude, such as Dooley Wilson's famous rendition of "As Time Goes By" in *Casablanca* (1942), generally are not considered film musicals. Nor by this definition does *American Graffiti* (1973) qualify as a musical, despite featuring a wall-to-wall sound track of period rock oldies, and even situating the source of the music within its narrative world as a radio broadcast by disc jockey Wolfman Jack, because there are no musical performances by any members of the film's ensemble cast. In George Lucas's nostalgic film about California high schoolers in the 1960s, the music does comment on the characters and their situations, but does not emanate from them. This makes all the difference between a musical film and – the subject of this book – the film musical.

Film musicals typically present their song-and/or-dance numbers in an imaginary space, even if this space is ostensibly a real location, and contained within a narrative framework. While other genres may construct a space distinctly their own – the frontier of the western, for example, as opposed to the historical West – only the musical depicts its space as charmed by the magic of performance, where anyone and

The Hollywood Film Musical, First Edition. Barry Keith Grant.
© 2012 Barry Keith Grant. Published 2012 by Blackwell Publishing Ltd.

everyone may burst into magnificent, breathtaking song and dance in order to give unhindered expression to their emotions. That this charmed space is "impossible" – that is, entirely cinematic – is made vividly clear early on in the genre's history in the climactic number of *Flying Down to Rio* (1933), when the chorines dance on the wings of airplanes supposedly for the admiring crowd on the ground below. This performance is not only improbable in terms of real aerodynamics, it also would be virtually impossible to witness from the perspective of the spectators within the film's narrative. Ernst Lubitsch's fantasy European kingdom of Sylvania in *The Love Parade* (1929), the magical town in *Brigadoon* (1954), and the enchanted land somewhere over the rainbow in *The Wizard of Oz* (1939) offer overt instances of this charmed space, but all musicals construct a world that is not Kansas anymore.

Rick Altman notes that the musical's privileged space is "a 'place' of transcendence where time stands still, where contingent concerns are stripped away to reveal the essence of things" (Altman, 1987: 66–7). As in the "green world" of Shakespeare, characters in musicals entering this charmed space undergo a transformation of the soul, coming in touch with their true feelings. In Woody Allen's *Everyone Says I Love You* (1996), in which the starring actors are palpably inept at singing and dancing, much as in the ABBA musical *Mamma Mia!* (2008), the characters and the actors who portray them transcend their own physical limitations through musical performance. This idea of the musical's transcendence of limitations is made explicit in Allen's climactic *pas-de-deux* with Goldie Hawn, who suddenly glides through the air along the River Seine, defying gravity, during their dance. Busby Berkeley's distinctive overhead shots showing his dancers forming changing abstract patterns, discussed in more detail in Chapters 1 and 3, provide a "God's-eye" point of view that is another manifestation of the musical's transcendent vision.

In a brief cameo role, director Samuel Fuller, known for the "raw," visceral style of his action movies, explained his film aesthetic in Jean-Luc Godard's *Pierrot Le Fou* (1965) by observing that "film is like a battleground: love, hate, action, violence, death... In one word, emotions." In musicals, emotion is articulated as motion and voice, dance and song. The genre thus consistently exploits movement and sound, the two basic elements of the film medium. Precisely for this reason musicals are, in Godard's own lovely phrase, "the idealization of cinema" (Godard, 1972: 87). In melodrama, although the characters' intense emotions are expressed through stylistic means (mise-en-scène, lighting, music), their feelings are often repressed; by contrast, in film musicals characters are uninhibited, expressing their emotion openly and unabashedly through song and dance. Gene Kelly's famous refrain in *Singin' in the Rain* (1952), "Gotta dance," refers not only to his own inclination in that specific film but to the genre as a whole. As the Lion says in *The Wizard of Oz* just before breaking into song, "It's been in me so long. I just have to let it out." In fact, because musicals give plastic shape to intangible emotion, the genre comes consistently closer than any other to Sergei Eisenstein's dream of an ideal expressionist cinema of such emotional saturation that "a gesture expands into gymnastics, [where] rage is expressed through a somersault" (Eisenstein, 1949: 7).

As a result of this "emotional saturation," the musical is the only genre that consistently violates the otherwise rigid logic of classic narrative cinema. In film musical, characters sing and dance to and for the camera, for the benefit of the film viewer rather than any ostensible audience within the film's story (although sometimes there is a surrogate audience present in the narrative). And they do so whether they are happy or sad, elated or despondent. While there may be an audience within a film musical's fictional world to provide narrative "motivation" for the musical interlude, clearly the actors are performing for an audience "beyond" the diegetic one – often signified in close-ups of actors while singing, their eyes fixed somewhere outside the frame – that is, for our pleasure as the viewers of the film. On occasion comedy films will break the "fourth wall," as when in, say, *Duck Soup* (1933) Groucho Marx addresses a wisecrack directly to the spectator every time he fails to get a ride in his motorcycle's sidecar; but only in film musicals do actors "address" the spectator for entire, often lengthy, sequences.

Moreover, the music accompanying singing or dancing performers in a film musical frequently comes from "nowhere" – from outside the diegesis or world of the film – another violation of the rules of realism that govern most other genres. In *Singin' in the Rain*, when Don Lockwood (Gene Kelly) adjusts the lighting and switches on a wind machine on an empty sound stage to set the mood before proclaiming his love for Kathy (Debbie Reynolds) in the song "You Were Meant for Me," the scene acknowledges the conventions of artificiality that characterize performance in film musicals even as it reveals and celebrates the artistry of the performers who are able to stir our romantic imaginations.

The film musical, perhaps more than any other genre, has always foregrounded its nature as generic construct and has thus demanded the greatest suspension of disbelief from the viewer. For characters to break out in song and/or dance is the most basic convention of the genre; and while it may be no less "real" than cowboys squaring off on Main Street at High Noon or the detective gathering all the suspects together in the drawing room to identify the killer, it seems more of a contrivance. It is for this very reason that German playwright Bertolt Brecht, who sought to create an "epic theatre" in which viewers would be distanced from the plot in order to encourage them to think more about the ideological implications of it, often relied on his characters breaking into song so as to achieve his "*Verfremdungseffekt*," or "alienation effect." For all most of us know, maybe cowboys did have that kind of showdown in the Wild West; but the sudden injection of song and dance into a narrative always announces the work's own artifice. Actors suddenly change their mode of action and become performers rather than the characters they were pretending to be.

This explicit address to viewers in the film musical is particularly striking given the social functions of popular music. As Simon Frith observes, popular music serves to enable "a particular sort of self definition" and to manage "the relationship between our public and private emotional lives" (Frith, 1987: 140–1). Popular cinema does no less. Film theorists see genres as cultural myths serving similar social and ideological functions in that they tend to take social debates and tensions and cast them into formulaic narratives, condensing them into dramatic conflicts between individual characters, heroes and villains, providing familiar stories that help us "narrativize" and so make sense of the large, abstract social forces that effect our lives. To the extent that genre films serve this ideological function, they define for us – or help us define, depending on one's point of view – our sense of self and our "proper" place within society. Film musicals, as this book will show, deploy both cinematic and musical elements for this purpose. Whereas westerns evolved from the dime novel, gangster films from pulp magazines and contemporary headlines, and horror movies from gothic novels, the film musical was a new form that developed along with Hollywood itself. If there is a previous form of popular culture that has been a significant shaping influence on the film musical, it is the popular music industry – of which film musicals themselves are a part.

Some national cinemas, such as those of Japan, Hong Kong, and Mexico, have produced film musicals, but with one exception, to be discussed below, no national cinema has produced any body of film musicals to compete with the sustained output of Hollywood. Important film-producing countries such as Italy, the Soviet Union, and China (in which the stage opera has been so crucial for entertainment and propaganda purposes) developed no notable tradition of film musicals. Soviet bloc countries during the Communist era produced very few musicals, as they did not fit comfortably within the prevailing approach of Socialist Realism. In France, René Clair experimented early on in France with

Sous les toits de Paris (1930) and *À nous la liberté* (1931). Later, during the New Wave period of the 1960s, Jacques Demy updated the operetta with several films, including *Les parapluies de Cherbourg* (1964), and periodically auteurs such as Alain Resnais (*La vie est un roman*, 1983), Chantal Akerman (*Golden Eighties*, aka *Window Shopping*, 1986), and François Ozon (*8 femmes*, 2002) have dabbled in the genre. But for the most part French directors have preferred dramatic genres such as the *policier* and film noir, the term itself coined by French critics. English cinema made many musicals, particularly during the 1930s; but with the exception of Michael Powell and Emeric Pressburger's *The Red Shoes* (1948) and *Tales of Hoffman* (1951), they were largely undistinguished quickies that are now mostly forgotten.

The only country other than the United States to have produced a sustained tradition of film musicals is India, which is also the largest film-producing country in the world. Within Indian cinema, the idea of a film musical is rather different than in the Hollywood tradition, but the genre's cultural impact has been even greater. About 90 percent of commercial feature films made in India have incorporated musical production numbers. Indian films typically have several song-and-dance sequences as part of their entertainment appeal, regardless of whether the genre is a romantic melodrama or a crime film. And just as the genres are disparate, so are the musical styles, mixing traditional Indian dance music with American jazz or Caribbean rhythms. In Indian popular culture, film music holds a prominent place, dominating sales of discs and tapes. Indian movie stars lip-sync the songs, and the actual vocalists, known as "playback singers," have, like Lata Mangeshkar, become recording stars in their own right.

India apart, in contrast to the cinemas of other countries, the centrality and importance of the film musical in the history of American cinema are clear when one considers the many stars who became famous primarily or initially through their roles in musicals. Some of the best known are Dick Powell, Judy Garland, Mickey Rooney, Shirley Temple, Betty Grable, Jeanette MacDonald and Nelson Eddy, Fred Astaire and Ginger Rogers, Gene Kelly, Deanna Durbin, and Cyd Charisse. In addition, many singers have crossed over from popular music to movies, from Frank Sinatra and Elvis to Madonna, David Bowie, and Ice T. Numerous writers, composers, choreographers, and a number of directors, among them Vincente Minnelli, Stanley Donen, Busby Berkeley, Ernst Lubitsch, and Baz Luhrmann, also became known for their work in the genre, the latter two producing important musicals on integrating into the Hollywood system after beginning their careers elsewhere.

Accordingly, this book focuses on film musicals produced in the United States. It begins with a concise history of the genre and an overview of the critical debates about it. These two chapters will provide the necessary contexts for the close readings of individual touchstone film musicals in the seven chapters to follow. Together, these analyses cover a variety of types of film musical and the history of the genre from its beginnings until today. Their range also allows for consideration of the various critical issues discussed in Chapter 2's critical overview. Throughout the goal has been to show how popular music and generic convention work within these film musicals to give them impressive aesthetic complexity and thematic depth.

CHAPTER 1
HISTORICAL OVERVIEW

Movies and music, two of the most important mass media in American culture, have intertwined histories from the outset. Movies began as part of the program in vaudeville shows and music halls. They interacted, as Charles Merrell Berg notes,

in the darkened, smoke-filled chambers of Bijou Dreams during the first decade of [the twentieth] century. Sitting beneath cataracts of flickering images, pianists ragged and riffed through the pop and standard tunes of the day. Sometimes their efforts helped underscore the drama. Mostly, however, their improvised medleys served to fill up the aural void and cover up the wisecracks and whirs from the projector. (Berg, 1978: 1)

Peter Wollen, meanwhile, begins his monograph on *Singin' in the Rain* (1952), generally acknowledged as one of the best film musicals of all time, by declaring that "[t]he history of cinema coincides with that of twentieth-century dance.... [A]s film itself developed as an art form, it intersected with dance to create a new phenomenon – film dance, dance created expressly for film, with camera, framing and editing in mind" (Wollen, 1992: 9). In the United States, the film musical genre, the site of the most intense interaction and synergy between movies and music, evolved from such diverse cultural forms as minstrelsy, vaudeville, Tin Pan Alley, and musical theater.

The Hollywood Film Musical, First Edition. Barry Keith Grant.
© 2012 Barry Keith Grant. Published 2012 by Blackwell Publishing Ltd.

Before Cinema

In the nineteenth century, minstrel shows were the most popular form of musical and comedy entertainment. Featuring white performers in black-face, the shows developed a formal structure with clearly established conventions built on comic racial stereotypes. Minstrel shows featured three distinct parts. In the first, the walkaround, the entire troupe came onto the stage, taking their seats in a semi-circular arrangement in unison upon the command from the master of ceremonies, or Interlocutor, "Gentlemen, be seated" and performing a selection of popular tunes. The two endmen, known as Mr Tambo (who played the tambourine) and Mr Bones (who played percussive castanets), engaged in comic banter with the dignified Interlocutor, who always sat in the middle of the semi-circle. The second part of the show, known as the olio, consisted of a medley of variety acts, and the finale was a series of comic skits, originally about plantation life but changed after the Civil War to parodies of classic and contemporary plays.

Minstrel shows toured the United States and Canada until as late as the middle of the twentieth century, when people began to regard them as racially embarrassing. Yet the influence of minstrelsy on popular music was enormous. Several classic blues singers such as Bessie Smith and Ma Rainey began their careers with black minstrel troupes. Some important songwriters also emerged from the tradition, including Dan Emmett, composer of "Dixie" (1859), originally written for the walkaround, and "Turkey in the Straw" (1861), among others; and Stephen Foster, composer of "Oh, Susannah" (1948), "Jeanie with the Light Brown Hair" (1854), "Beautiful Dreamer" (1863), and "My Old Kentucky Home" (1853), which was originally introduced by The Christy Minstrels. These songs, played in white middle-class homes across the United States on parlor pianos, were known as "Ethiopian Songs" – a euphemistic term that, like record companies' later segregation of black music on "sepia" series and the like, revealed the dynamics of race that have informed so much of the country's popular music.

In popular film, the influence of minstrelsy may be seen directly in early film musicals starring Al Jolson and Eddie Cantor. Both popular singers had performed in blackface on the stage and then brought their "burnt cork" personas to Hollywood: Jolson in *The Jazz Singer* (1927), the first hit film musical; and Cantor in *Whoopee!* (1930) and *Palmy Days* (1931), the first two musicals on which Busby Berkeley worked. (Berkeley is discussed further below and in Chapter 3.) Later in the 1930s, blackface numbers included Fred Astaire's "Bojangles in Harlem" in *Swing Time* (1936) and Harpo's "All God's Chillun Got Rhythm" in the Marx Brothers' *A Day at the Races* (1937). Even into the 1940s, Bing Crosby sang in blackface in the "Abraham" number of *Holiday Inn* (1942) and for "Ac-cent-tchu-ate the the Positive" in the war musical *Here Comes the Waves* (1944). More recently, Spike Lee's *Bamboozled* (2000) satirically explored the iconography and cultural legacy of minstrelsy in American culture.

Minstrelsy evolved into "the basic components of all American stage entertainment. The minstrel line evolved into what became known as the 'coon show' before emerging as revue, the olio developed into vaudeville, and the concluding sketch inspired both burlesque and the musical comedy" (Parkinson, 2007: 4). Further, the demand for and sales of sheet music for many of the songs featured in minstrel shows helped significantly to stimulate the growth of the popular music industry in the United States. Until the invention of the phonograph and the commercial availability of recordings, sheet music was the primary medium for the retailing of popular music. Hit songs could sell millions of copies. In 1902, Harry von Tilzer's "On a Sunday Afternoon" sold 10,000 copies in one day in a single New York department store (Kingman, 1979: 268).

In 1897, the pianola, or player piano, was introduced to the consumer market and was very popular through the 1920s. Piano rolls, paper rolls with perforations in them, were inserted into the instrument which, when turned, moved the keys to play a song. Piano rolls featured the popular songs of the day, including those of such important songwriters as George Gershwin. Player pianos allowed people to have piano music in their parlors even if they could not actually play the instrument, and for music to be played in bars and other venues that could not afford a live pianist, furthering the dissemination of popular songs. This innovation was accompanied by "song-slides" which began to appear in vaudeville acts from 1907 and showed song lyrics projected on a screen as they were being sung by a live performer (Burns, 1988: 221).

Thomas Edison invented the phonograph in 1877, but it was with Victor's introduction in 1906 of the Victrola, the first phonograph designed as furniture, that music truly became a consumable commodity. The phonograph, said media guru Marshall McLuhan, was a "music hall without walls" (McLuhan, 1964: 248). As philosopher Evan Eisenberg writes, with the phonograph and records, "[n]ow the Symphony of a Thousand could play to an audience of one. Now a man could hear nocturnes at breakfast, vespers at noon, and the Easter Oratorio on Chanukah. He could do his morning crossword to the 'One O'Clock

Jump' and make love right through the St Matthew Passion" (Eisenberg, 1987: 29). Music, in other words, was now a thing that could be "owned" and "used." Popular music gained further portability in the 1950s with the introduction of the transistor radio, a process that would continue toward the end of the century with audiotape cassettes and walkmans, and then digital technology, which has offered a variety of personal listening devices and the ability to access music through the internet.

As with pop music makers today releasing their own CDs, early twentieth-century songwriters churned out songs in the hope of scoring big with a hit. Pluggers publicized the songs the publishers were promoting as potential sheet music hits by playing them in music and department stores, and paying vaudeville singers to sing them in their acts. Irving Berlin, Jerome Kern, and George Gershwin were among the important songwriters who began as song pluggers before composing their own songs for Broadway musicals (Kingman, 1979: 268). Many of these songwriters worked in Tin Pan Alley, along with the pluggers, publishers, and, later, record companies. Named after a street in New York (its actual location changed over the years), Tin Pan Alley originated as a journalist's vivid phrase to describe the din of all the composers' pianos rattling through the open windows of their offices. It has since become synonymous with the institution of popular music itself, both as an industry and as a conservative ideology (see the discussions of *Woodstock* [1970] in Chapter 7 and *Pennies from Heaven* [1981] in Chapter 9).

The songwriters wrote first for vaudeville and then musical theater. Vaudeville became a national pastime beginning in the 1870s, particularly with urban working-class and immigrant audiences. American composers such as George M. Cohan (*Little Johnny Jones*, 1904) and Victor Herbert (*Babes in Toyland*, 1903) began to weld musical numbers to narrative, setting the foundation for the film musical. Impresario Florenz Ziegfeld created a revue program known as the "Follies" that was an annual Broadway event for two decades. Ziegfeld's "Follies" featured such performers as W.C. Fields, Will Rogers, Eddie Cantor, and Fanny Brice (the subject of *Funny Girl* [1968] with Barbra Streisand) and a dazzling chorus line. Similar musical revues followed, including Earl Carroll's "Vanities" and George White's "Scandals."

With the arrival of sound film in 1927, several of Ziegfeld's productions, including *Whoopee!*, were adapted for the big screen. Movies, in the words of J. Hoberman, offered "Ziegfeld for the masses," with film prints distributed around the country to the movie palaces of the big cities and small theaters in rural communities alike (Hoberman, 1993: 11). Many film musicals were adaptations of theatrical musicals, or contained songs borrowed from them. In turn, many performers, choreographers, composers, lyricists, and directors moved from musical theater to Hollywood musicals after the arrival of sound. Jerome Kern and Oscar Hammerstein II's *Show Boat* was adapted for the screen no fewer than three times – in 1929, 1936, and 1951. *Till the Clouds Roll By* (1946), a musical biopic about Kern, begins with the debut performance of this milestone play in December 1927.

The Arrival of Sound

Researchers beginning with Thomas Edison, the American inventor of both the motion picture camera and phonograph, had been experimenting with ways to combine or synchronize sound with film images for years, but early efforts were met largely with indifference from the film industry because of the technical problems involved. Early technology, which relied on sound-on-disc systems (records that would be played at the same time as a movie was projected), was problematic and unreliable. Things changed dramatically, however, when Warner Bros, then a second-rank studio looking for a competitive edge, collaborated with Western Electric, a subsidiary of AT&T, on a sound-on-film system that Warners dubbed Vitaphone. The studio initially had the idea of "canning" musical scores for their movies, which would allow them to have orchestral accompaniment for their productions, something that only the major studios could afford live for their big releases in first-run theaters; but it did not take long for the Brothers Warner to realize that talking pictures would be more than a passing fad.

Opening in October 1927, Warners' *The Jazz Singer*, often cited as the first feature-length sound film and the first film musical, was a sensational hit (Plate 1). The movie, which featured established Broadway star Al Jolson, was in fact mostly a silent film – it even included intertitles – with seven musical sequences added, including the signature Jolson tunes "Mammy" and "Waiting for the Robert E. Lee." The story of a young Jewish man who abandons his future as a cantor and, against his father's wishes, becomes a popular singer was the stuff of melodrama; but it was the talking and singing that audiences remembered. Jolson's famous ad-libbed line "You ain't heard nothin' yet" seemed to announce the arrival not only of *The Jazz Singer* but of the musical genre itself. The film's box-office success, as well as that of *The Lights of New York* in 1928, a Warner Bros' two-reeler that was expanded to become the first all-taking feature,

PLATE 1 Al Jolson as Jakie Rabinowitz in *The Jazz Singer* (Alan Crosland, 1927; Producer: Darryl F. Zanuck).

allowed the studio to undergo rapid expansion and become a fully integrated major by the end of the decade.

Audiences clamored for talkies, and, as a result, in a mere three years, by the end of the decade, musicals had become a staple Hollywood product. By the middle of 1929, 25 percent of movies in production were musicals (Hoberman, 1993: 15), and, according to one historian of the genre, "[t]he studios turned out musicals like sausages" (Stern, 1974: 19). As Hollywood pundits observed, Greta Garbo and Rin Tin Tin were the only stars who were not taking singing lessons. The rush of the studios to convert to sound and to produce musicals to exploit the new technology is treated humorously in the plot of *Singin' in the Rain*: when the attempt to make a sound film with silent film star Lina Lamont (Jean Hagan) results in disaster because of her thick Brooklyn accent, Don Lockwood (Gene Kelly) and Cosmo Brown (Donald O'Connor) save the film by changing the romantic adventure they were making, "The Dueling Cavalier," into a musical entitled "The Dancing Cavalier" and dubbing Lamont's voice with that of Kathy Selden (Debbie Reynolds). One hilarious scene shows some of the problems filmmakers at first faced with the new technology, which required that cameras be "blimped" in order for their motors not to be picked up by microphone.

Although tie-ins between movies and music began as early as 1918, when the song "Mickey" was commissioned for Mack Sennett's film of that name (Hall and Neale, 2010: 84), the coming of sound significantly increased the demand for songs in Hollywood. Jolson's recording of "Sonny Boy" for *The Singing Fool* (1928), another part-talkie musical that was his follow-up to *The Jazz Singer*, sold 370,000 records in the first three months of the film's release and ultimately achieved combined sales of over a million discs and sheet-music copies. All the studios, needing a consistent supply of music, moved to acquire music publishing companies: Warner Bros, for example, bought M. Witmark & Sons, while Paramount established its own music division and commissioned songs from independent songwriters such as Irving Berlin (Hall and Neale, 2010: 85). As one journalist wrote in 1929, "It is now a question as to which has absorbed which. Is the motion picture industry a subsidiary of the music publishing business – or have film producers gone into the business of making songs?" (Kreuger, 1975: 56). As Broadway already "was well in decline" in the early 1930s, many Broadway composers, including Berlin, Cole Porter, Rodgers and Hart, and George and Ira Gershwin, happily came to work in Hollywood (Hoberman, 1993: 9). Anticipating synergistic potential, the studios also moved into the medium of radio. Warner Bros, for example, established radio stations across the country, and Paramount acquired 50 percent of the stock of the newly formed Columbia Broadcasting System (CBS) (Hall and Neale, 2010: 85).

The first director to distinguish himself in the genre of the film musical was Ernst Lubitsch, a Jewish-German director who came to Hollywood in 1923. Lubitsch made a series of musicals and comedies that combined sophistication and sex. His first, *The Love Parade* (1929), set in the imaginary European kingdom of Sylvania, combined French star Maurice Chevalier and Jeanette MacDonald. In 1932, Lubitsch reunited Chevalier and MacDonald in *One Hour with You* (co-directed by George Cukor), a remake of his own earlier hit comedy *The Marriage Circle* (1924). Another of Lubitsch's comedies, *Ninotchka* (1939), was remade as *Silk Stockings* in 1957 by Rouben Mamoulian, who in the 1930s had followed Lubitsch's lead and paired Chevalier and MacDonald in *Love Me Tonight* (1932). Lubitsch's films were seen as representing a continental "touch"– a "counterpoint between sadness and gaiety" (Sarris, 1968: 66) – that set them apart from the typically more straightforwardly upbeat American romantic comedies and musicals.

Finally, animated cartoons, part of a regular program in movie theaters during the studio era, relied heavily on popular music. The names of cartoon series such as Disney's "Silly Symphonies," Walter Lantz's "Swing

Symphonies," Max Fleischer's "Screen Songs" and "Car-Tunes," and Warners' "Looney Tunes" and "Merrie Melodies," suggest the importance they placed on popular music. As Roy Prendergast points out, cartoons are usually no more than a few minutes in length, and events in them tend to transpire at breakneck pace, so that musical technique gravitates toward an "aphoristic brevity" (Prendergast, 1987: 172). The musical scores of cartoons were generally pastiches of popular and folk tunes easily recognizable by viewers. Their basic function was to provide sound effects and "atmosphere" for the animated action, rather than making the music a contributing element of an artistic whole, and thus it is not by accident that the same practice in classic Hollywood film scoring is called "mickey-mousing."

Depression-Era Musicals

As the industry quickly converted to sound, several distinct subgenres of the musical emerged. Revue musicals, containing a loosely strung together series of acts with minimal plot, carried over the variety format of vaudeville. *The King of Jazz* (1930), for example, is structured around a series of songs, dances, and comedy sketches by popular stars of the day introduced by bandleader Paul Whiteman; the various numbers and acts have no relationship or connection apart from Whiteman's claim that many of the disparate performances have combined in the great "melting pot of music" to create the new sound of jazz. *The Hollywood Revue of 1929* featured almost every star in MGM's famed lineup (as well as the debut of Nacio Herb Brown's "Singin' in the Rain," made famous decades later with MGM's release of the film of the same title), while Warner Bros trotted out many of its stars the same year for *Show of Shows* (1929) and Paramount did the same with *Paramount on Parade* (1930).

Operettas also were popular, with Sigmund Romberg and Oscar Hammerstein's *The Desert Song* (1929), Warners' debut "100% all talking, 100% all singing" operetta, starring John Boles and Myrna Loy, the first to be filmed. The most popular operettas were a string of eight films starring Nelson Eddy and Jeanette MacDonald, from *Naughty Marietta* (1935), an adaptation of a Victor Herbert operetta, to *I Married an Angel* (1942). By 1934, the form was already the target of parody in *Babes in Toyland* with comic duo Stan Laurel and Oliver Hardy, and was coming to seem dated to audiences during the Swing Era.

However, another musical genre, the backstage musical, or show-within-the film formula, proved much more successful and has provided the most durable narrative framework for the musical film because it offers a reason or pretext for the presence of production numbers. MGM's *Broadway Melody* (1929) was a backstage musical about two sisters seeking fame in the theater. The film won the Academy Award for Best Picture and established the formula for many of the backstage musicals to follow. Although the backstage format declined with the rise of the "integrated musical," wherein the production numbers seemed to emerge from narrative and dialogue, it continued through the war years and informs such later and otherwise different musicals as *Moulin Rouge!* (2001) and *8 Mile* (2003) with rap singer Eminem.

By the early 1930s, Warner Bros was producing a remarkable cycle of backstage musicals, many featuring the musical choreography of Busby Berkeley, including *42nd Street* (1933) (Plate 2), *Gold Diggers of 1933* (1933, discussed in Chapter 3), *Footlight Parade* (1933), and *Dames* (1934). The songs for many of the Warners' film musicals were written by Al Dubin and Harry Warren, veteran Tin Pan Alley songwriters brought together by the studio's head of production, Darryl F. Zanuck. With their

PLATE 2 Director Julian Marsh (Warner Baxter) rehearsing his cast in the backstage musical *42nd Street* (Lloyd Bacon/Busby Berkeley, 1933; Producer: Darryl F. Zanuck).

upbeat messages of group effort and success, as well as their visual lavishness offering a stark contrast to the realities of economic impoverishment, these musicals were very popular with Depression-era audiences. In Andrew Sarris' words, "Berkeley's spectacle effects possessed a giddy, vertiginous, disorienting charm ... [that had] their time and place in the depths of the Depression when the difference between quality and quantity did not seem too important" (Sarris, 1968: 172). As Joseph B. Craft of Bell Laboratories declares in the 1926 Vitaphone short "The Voice from the Screen," Warner Bros had put into *42nd Street* "stars, girls, beauty, and talent in lavish quantities."

Berkeley moved to Warner Bros from MGM in 1933, and over the course of the next six years choreographed and/or directed nineteen musicals at the studio, some of which were among the most popular of the decade. Berkeley came to choreography during his military service, where he organized stylized parade drills, and then in the theater, where he designed the dances for many shows. Coming to Hollywood, Berkeley knew nothing about film production and so worked, unusually, with only one camera. Despite his lack of knowledge about the medium of cinema, he realized that staging musical numbers for film "was entirely different than on the stage. In pictures you see everything through the eye of the camera. Unlike the theatre, where your eyes can roam at will, the director and his cameramen decide where the viewer will look" (Thomas and Terry, 1973: 24). Thus, in Berkeley's musical numbers the confining proscenium of the stage gives way to the fluid frame of the motion picture image, and dances are choreographed for the ideal, changing point of view of a film spectator rather than for the static position of a traditional theatergoer. As discussed in the context of *Gold Diggers of 1933* in Chapter 3, Berkeley was the first to use close-ups of individual chorines, and also was famous for his distinctive bird's-eye-view shots of the dancers creating geometric patterns that sway and reconfigure.

The only series of film musicals to rival Berkeley's in the 1930s was RKO's cycle of romantic musical comedies with Fred Astaire and Ginger Rogers. In nine films for the studio, Astaire and Rogers seemed to dance their way through the Depression. The pair had supporting roles behind stars Dolores del Rio and Gene Raymond in *Flying Down to Rio* (1933), and the following year they first starred in *The Gay Divorcee* (1934). (They returned for a reprise a decade later with *The Barkleys of Broadway* [1949] for MGM.) Five of the nine pictures, including *Top Hat* (1935), examined in Chapter 4, were directed by Mark Sandrich; three of them featured scores by Irving Berlin, with others composed by Kern and Gershwin, and all introduced at least one song that has become a standard. Astaire, who choreographed his own dances, often with the collaboration of Hermes Pan, preferred to show them in long takes, with as little editing as possible, in sharp distinction to Berkeley, whose musical numbers rely heavily on editing.

The Astaire–Rogers musicals all featured variations of the same basic plot in which the two stars are initially attracted to each other but unable to come together owing to some comic misunderstanding; the conflict is resolved when the couple's differences are reconciled, generally through the mediating power of musical performance, resulting in their union. Rogers makes this clear enough to Astaire in *The Gay Divorcee* when she sings to him about "The Continental" (the first song to win an Academy Award for Best Original Song) in which "You tell of your love while you dance." Their romantic dilemmas, played out in luxurious settings like plush hotels and ocean liners where money seemed to be irrelevant, provided another form of escapist fare for Depression audiences. The image of Astaire riding the rails in *Swing Time*, like so many forgotten men in the 1930s, but here in top hat and tails, attests to his sophisticated appeal for contemporary audiences (R. Wood, 1979: 29).

The Astaire–Rogers films worked so well because the two performers were equal partners in the dance numbers, neither one dominating the screen when they danced together. In the climax of *Shall We Dance* (1937), Astaire sings "They Can't Take That Away from Me" amid a sea of women all wearing identical Ginger Rogers masks. When Rogers is told that "If he couldn't dance with you, he'd dance with images of you," she joins the chorus on stage, momentarily reveals her true self, and then makes Astaire search her out by unmasking and rejecting all the others before they can dance alone. The number choreographs their destiny as dancing partners.

World War II

With the United States' entry into World War II in December 1941, everyone from Abbott and Costello to the Bowery Boys joined in, helping to boost the morale of troops overseas as well as on the home front in their movies. Even Humphrey Bogart's familiar gangster type, normally a social outcast, now turned his attention to fighting Fifth Columnists in *All Through the Night* (1941). As in *Hollywood Canteen* (1944), the backstage narrative moved the show from Broadway to the new locale of the USO tour or benefit show to sell war bonds. The film musical was in the doldrums in the late 1930s, both in popularity and production, but that changed abruptly with the country's entry into the war, as it became "the dominant film genre of wartime Hollywood" (Woll, 1983: ix). In 1943, during the height of the war, 40 percent of the films produced in Hollywood were musicals. Stylistically, however, wartime musicals tended to be considerably less extravagant than the Busby Berkeley spectacles of the preceding decade as Americans were called upon to reduce material consumption as part of the war effort.

Walt Disney's Donald Duck cartoon *Der Fuehrer's Face* (1942), which won an Oscar for Best Short Animated Film, is unambiguous in its patriotic message. The cartoon was made after Oliver Wallace's song, which explicitly mocks Hitler and his "new world order," was first popularized by the novelty band Spike Jones and His City Slickers. In the cartoon, Donald Duck has a nightmare that he is living under the Nazi regime, forced to work on a munitions assembly line until he has a nervous breakdown. Finally awaking from his nightmare in his own bed in his stars-and-stripes pajamas, Donald kisses the replica of the Statue of Liberty on the window sill and, as he throws a tomato at a picture of Hitler, says, "I'm glad to be a citizen of the United States of America" as the cartoon ends.

During the war, the film musical, so often seen as escapist fantasy, was likewise explicit in its patriotic fervor. Before the bombing of Pearl Harbor, the popular sentiment of the country was non-interventionist, and Americans needed to be convinced to "band together" in the common war effort. Warner Bros' *Yankee Doodle Dandy* (1942), about composer George M. Cohan, perhaps the most successful composer of patriotic songs during World War I, was among the most overtly propagandistic musicals of the period. As Frank Capra would do in the series of overtly propagandistic *Why We Fight* (1942–5) films made for the Office of War Information, *Yankee Doodle Dandy* combined patriotic melodies, in this case Cohan's, on the sound track with iconographic images of American national mythology and history. At one point President Roosevelt presents Cohan (James Cagney, whose performance won him a Best Actor Oscar) with the Congressional Medal of Honor, telling him that "your songs were weapons as strong as cannons and rifles in World War I."

The film's music includes "You're a Grand Old Flag" and "Over There," perhaps the most popular of patriotic songs with soldiers during World War I. In addition, Cohan's play *Little Nellie Kelly* (1922) was transformed by MGM into the musical *Babes on Broadway* (1941), with Judy Garland and Mickey Rooney and directed by Berkeley. "Over There" also was included in *Four Jills and a Jeep* (1944), and another Cohan song, "Give My Regards to Broadway," was used in *The Great American*

Broadcast (1941) (Woll, 1983: 61). The invocation of Cohan was intended to link the patriotic sentiment of the earlier war with the new one. As the war progressed, though, Irving Berlin emerged as the great new patriotic songwriter. *Holiday Inn* included Berlin's "Song of Freedom," and the following year *This is the Army* (1943) featured songs such as "Oh, How I Hate to Get Up in the Morning," "How about a Cheer for the Navy" and the enshrined "God Bless America."

Nostalgic invocations of America's past were also invoked in other biopics of famous composers, including Stephen Foster (*Swanee River,* 1939) and George Gershwin (*Rhapsody in Blue,* 1945), as well in other musicals like *For Me and My Gal* (1942) and *Minstrel Man* (1944). Betty Grable, famous for her pin-up pose known as "the legs that won the war," lifted the morale of American servicemen with several charming, nostalgic musicals, including *Tin Pan Alley* (1940), *Sweet Rosie O'Grady* (1943), and *Coney Island* (1943), that reminded soldiers what they were fighting for overseas. Further, old Broadway shows such as *Irene* (1940), *No, No Nanette* (1941), and *DuBarry was a Lady* (1943) were revived and made as movies. The nostalgic emphasis of these pictures appealed to viewers' feelings of national pride and tradition at a time when their resolve was being severely tested.

The government established a "Good Neighbor Policy" toward Central and South America for the purpose of encouraging countries there not to support the Axis powers, and Hollywood participated in the campaign by making a cycle of musicals set south of the border. The studios also realized that the potential audience in South American countries would compensate to some extent for the European markets lost to Hollywood during the war. If the film musical after *Flying Down to Rio* had largely ignored the existence of South America, which had contributed such dances as the mambo and conga to American popular music, now the studios released *Down Argentine Way* (1940), *That Night in Rio* (1941), *Weekend in Havana* (1941), and *They Met in Argentina* (1941), among others. Latin performers Desi Arnaz, Cesar Romero, and Carmen Miranda rose to stardom during this period. Despite the good intention of these films, however, they were often resented by Latin audiences because of their characteristic stereotyping.

The "Golden Age"

While the revue and backstage formats dominated the film musical during the war, Broadway musicals began moving toward combining musical numbers with drama rather than comedy in *Oklahoma!* (1943) and *Carousel* (1945) by composer Richard Rodgers and lyricist Oscar Hammerstein, both of which were adapted as film musicals in 1955 and 1956, respectively. In the same decade, producer Arthur Freed approached the film musical as an organic whole, tying the music to the book, the production numbers to the narrative. Freed produced more than thirty quality musicals between 1939 and 1960, mostly for MGM, and also was a lyricist (he wrote the words for "Singin' in the Rain," among others). In Freed's film musicals, beginning with his first, *The Wizard of Oz*, in 1939, the musical numbers tend to arise out of the story and even advance the plot rather than merely interrupt it, as was too frequently the case in the genre previously.

According to many film historians, the musicals produced by Freed represent the height of the genre's Golden Age, roughly from the end of World War II through the 1950s. Freed's unit at MGM included, among others, performers Fred Astaire, Gene Kelly, Judy Garland, and Frank Sinatra; directors Stanley Donen and Vincente Minnelli; choreographer Michael Kidd; and screen and songwriting duo Betty Comden and Adolph Green. These artists, along with many others, were collectively responsible for such recognized classics as *The Wizard of Oz*, *Cabin in the Sky* (1943), *Meet Me in St Louis* (1944), *On the Town* (1949), *An American in Paris* (1951), *Singin' in the Rain*, *The Band Wagon* (1953), *It's Always Fair Weather* (1955), and *Silk Stockings*, among others. Despite their different settings, these film musicals all integrate their narratives and musical numbers in more sophisticated ways than had been the case previously in the genre.

Producers Joe Pasternak (*Anchors Aweigh*, 1945; *Love Me or Leave Me*, 1955) and Jack Cummings (*Three Little Words*, 1950; *Seven Brides for Seven Brothers*, 1954) also were responsible for musicals at MGM, and some of them were also successful at the box office. Other studios, too, continued to make musicals: comedian Danny Kaye starred in a series of popular film musicals for other studios, including Warner Bros (*The Inspector General*, 1949) and Paramount (*The Court Jester*, 1956); and Doris Day made a number of musicals for Warner Bros, among them *April in Paris* (1952) with Ray Bolger, *Calamity Jane* (1953) with Howard Keel, and *Young at Heart* (1954) with Frank Sinatra, before moving on to the series of romantic comedies for which she is most remembered. But the Freed Unit musicals have proven the most popular with audiences and the most thematically rich for critics.

Backstage musicals typically delay their musical sequences, or at least the most spectacular of them, until the climax of the narrative, which is the successful mounting of the show. Freed's integrated musicals, by contrast, distribute the musical sequences in the narrative more evenly. Many of them "discover" song and dance — this potential for emotional intensity — in apparently mundane situations. In *The Band Wagon*, for example, Astaire performs "A Shine on Your Shoes," enabling him, early on, to acknowledge the loneliness he feels upon his return to Broadway, which he thinks has passed him by. The act of having his shoes shined turns into a dance and song that develop from the rhythms of the shoeshine man's buffing cloth (Plate 3). Similarly, in *It's Always Fair Weather*, Doug Hallerton (Dan Dailey), disgruntled about the superficial banter in the advertising agency where he works, finds rhythms in his colleagues' jargon ("Situation-wise and saturation-wise") and turns it into a cathartic song and dance. *On the Town*, meanwhile, opens on location on the docks of New York, where it finds music in the noble labor of the longshoremen.

In the postwar period, Gene Kelly emerged as MGM's leading star of musicals. Kelly was an actor, dancer, choreographer, and director, and a key figure in the musical's golden age. Having established himself on

PLATE 3 Fred Astaire as Tony Hunter dances to "A Shine on Your Shoes" in *The Band Wagon* (Vincente Minnelli, 1953; Producer: Arthur Freed).

Broadway starring in the stage musical *Pal Joey*, Kelly was brought to Hollywood by the producer David Selznick. His film debut was in Berkeley's *For Me and My Gal* with Judy Garland in 1942. After appearing in several minor musicals, such as *Thousands Cheer* (1943), where he dances with a mop, and some undistinguished dramatic features, Kelly was lent to Columbia to co-star with Rita Hayworth in *Cover Girl* (1944).

As a result of *Cover Girl*'s success, MGM cast Kelly in *Anchors Aweigh* (1945), for which he created his own dance routines, including the famous duet with the animated character of Jerry the mouse, earning him an Academy Award nomination for best actor. At MGM Kelly starred in *The Pirate* (1948), *On the Town, An American in Paris, Singin' in the Rain, Brigadoon* (1954), and *It's Always Fair Weather*, among others. *An American in Paris* won six Oscars, and Kelly, who was co-director, lead star, and choreographer, received a Special Academy Award for his "extreme versatility as an actor, singer, director, and dancer, but specifically for his brilliant achievements in the art of choreography on film." In the latter part of his career, Kelly directed the big-budget musical *Hello, Dolly!* (1969), starring Barbra Streisand, and was introduced to a new generation of moviegoers as the on-screen host of the compilation films *That's Entertainment* (1974) and *That's Entertainment II* (1976). Both culled the best musical numbers from the MGM film library and were hits at the box office. The first of the two films became MGM's top-grossing musical ever, earning just over $19 million (Parkinson, 2007: 50). By contrast, and sadly, Kelly's last singing and dancing film appearance, in *Xanadu* (1980) with Olivia Newton-John, was a box-office flop.

Whereas Fred Astaire was the master of ballroom dancing, Kelly, with his background in sports, brought a more muscular style to dance in film, popularizing ballet and modern dance for movie audiences. Some of his dances deliberately impose physical obstacles that warrant impressive athleticism and strength, like the climactic gymnastic dance with the Nicholas Brothers at the end of *The Pirate*. Considered in detail in Chapter 5, *The Pirate* featured Kelly as a romantic swashbuckling figure, allowing ample opportunity for the display of his athletic abilities. In *It's Always Fair Weather*, co-directed by Kelly and fellow choreographer Stanley Donen, Kelly, along with Michael Kidd and Dan Dailey, dance on a studio street with metal garbage can lids on their feet, and in *Singin' in the Rain*, also co-directed with Donen, he dances in a studio downpour, splashing his feet in holes arranged in advance to catch the rain in puddles (Plate 4). Kelly also brought a change from the upper-class image of tuxedo and top hat associated with Astaire that

PLATE 4 Gene Kelly as Don Lockwood performs the title tune in *Singin' in the Rain* (Stanley Donen and Gene Kelly, 1952; Producer: Arthur Freed).

characterized the genre in the 1930s, tending instead in his films to dress in casual, everyday clothes.

Just as Kelly's image was distinctly different from Astaire's, so, too, was his approach to dance on film. Kelly experimented with the expressive elements of cinema, including lighting, camera techniques, and special

Diff. bet. Kelly + Astaire

effects. Some of his best dances, like the one with Jerry the cartoon mouse, were only possible on film. While Astaire had dramatically changed the musical from Berkeley's emphasis on camera techniques by relying on full shots of the dancers' bodies and employing long takes, Kelly freed up the camera once again but, unlike Berkeley, focused on the bodies of the individual dancers rather than an entire chorus. In the title dance of *Singin' in the Rain*, for example, the camera generally moves to follow Kelly as he dances, but there are also times when the camera moves in a complementary fashion, coming in for a close-up as he sings "put a smile on your face" or craning up and away when he leaves the sidewalk and dances in the middle of the street.

Postwar Decline

Toward the end of the 1950s, the film musical suffered a surprising decline in production and popularity. In 1943, during World War II, Hollywood studios released sixty-five musicals, but a decade later the number was down to thirty-eight, and in 1963 a mere four musicals were released (Dowdy, 1975: 123). Television, which was introduced commercially in the United States in 1947, had by the 1950s become serious entertainment competition for Hollywood. Some television shows were hosted by Hollywood stars who had migrated to the new medium. Dick Powell, for example, the romantic lead of several of Berkeley's Warner Bros musicals in the 1930s, hosted *Zane Grey Theater* (CBS, 1956–61), while Bob Hope (star of several musical comedy "Road to" movies with Bing Crosby and Dorothy Lamour in the 1940s), Donald O'Connor (*Singin' in the Rain*), and Eddie Cantor (early Busby Berkeley musicals) were among the rotating hosts of *The Colgate Comedy Hour* (1950–5) on NBC. Also, musical performers were siphoned from the big screen into popular variety shows such as NBC's *The George Gobel Hour* (1954–60) and, of course, CBS's *The Ed Sullivan Show*, a Sunday-night American institution from 1948 to 1971 and itself the subject of mocking reverential humor in *Bye Bye Birdie* (1963).

Partly in response to the new rival medium, Hollywood embraced technology as yet unavailable to television, especially the use of color and the widescreen format. The wider image was particularly appropriate for the lavish scale of many film musicals, as were the exaggerated hues of Technicolor for the idealized fantasies of the musical's production numbers. *An American in Paris*, for example, exploits color in its production design inspired by French Impressionist paintings, while the climactic twelve-minute "Girl Hunt" ballet in *The Band Wagon*, an homage to hard-boiled detective fiction, is rendered in appropriately garish colors that accent the pulp quality of the novels.

By the late 1930s, rising costs had been making the production of lavish musicals increasingly prohibitive. After World War II, the big bands that had so dominated the popular music scene became economically unfeasible, and small combos began electrifying their instruments and playing uptempo rhythm 'n' blues to compensate for fewer musicians. Similarly, the studios found it difficult to keep fully staffed orchestras on the payroll (Hall and Neale, 2010: 184). Yet it was not this economic constraint that threatened the genre's survival. After Busby Berkeley left Warner Bros, his later musicals at MGM, beginning in 1939 with *Babes in Arms*, showed that, even with greatly reduced budgets, musicals could still be both innovative and commercially successful. People may have had more reason to sing in the rain in the immediate postwar period than during the tensions of the Cold War in the 1950s and 1960s, but the difficulties of the Depressions and the war years had stimulated the musical rather than stifled it.

Rather, the rapid decline of musicals in the late 1950s was at least partly the result of an ever-widening gap between the music used in the movies the studios were making and the music an increasing percentage of the nation was actually listening to – namely, the new rock 'n' roll (Grant, 1986: 199ff.). During the 1950s, the teenager emerged as a specific demographic that was a newly targeted audience by movie makers, as suggested by developments in other genres during the period such as the cycle of horror films that included *I Was a Teenage Werewolf* (1957), *Teenage Monster* (1957), *Teenage Caveman* (1958), and *I Was a Teenage Frankenstein* (1958).

Frank Tashlin's *The Girl Can't Help It* (1956) was the first big-budget Hollywood musical with rock 'n' roll music. The movie, featuring a series of great rock performances by Little Richard, Gene Vincent, Eddie Cochran, and Fats Domino, begins with a prologue in which star Tom Ewell appears and, speaking directly to the camera, explains that the film we are about to see is a story about music – "not the music of long ago, but the music that expresses the culture, the refinement, the polite grace of the present day." On the word "culture," the camera pans right to bring a jukebox into center frame with Ewell; at the end of the sentence, Little Richard's raucous title tune begins and the camera tracks into the jukebox, which glows with a red-hot intensity – imagery especially resonant during the Cold War. The song overwhelms the more sedate classical music that precedes it – "Roll Over, Beethoven," as Chuck Berry sang in his hit song of the same name that year – as well as Ewell's adult, authoritative narrator.

This pre-credit sequence of *The Girl Can't Help It* is a telling expression of the generation gap engendered by the new postwar youth culture of the 1950s. As David Ehrenstein and Bill Reed put it:

> With its concerns of sex and speed, instead of the "June, moon and spoon" of their parents' music, rock was a perfect music for the atomic era – its goading orgiastic sound made all the more poignant by the possibility of oblivion's imminence. Everytime [*sic*] a parent got unnerved over phonographs blaring out "that noise" their offspring could well have reminded them of an even bigger noise that was totally an adult responsibility. The Big Beat may have seemed dangerous to mom and pop, but it couldn't hold a candle to the Big Bang. (Ehrenstein and Reed, 1982: 15)

In the late 1960s, after the British invasion had made rock music even more popular, such musicals as *Doctor Dolittle* (1967), *Hello, Dolly!*, *Paint Your Wagon* (1969), and *Goodbye, Mr Chips* (1969) were commercially unsuccessful while, by contrast, the two Beatles films directed by Richard Lester, *A Hard Day's Night* (1964) and *Help!* (1965), brought an invigorating energy to the genre and were huge box-office successes. In the early 1970s, with the exception of *Fiddler on the Roof* (1971), more traditional musicals, such as *1776* (1972) and *The Little Prince* (1974), did not fare well commercially. But *Woodstock,* discussed in Chapter 7, a documentary about the legendary 1969 rock concert, and *American Graffiti* (1973), with its sound track of rock oldies, were major hits at the box office. The youth audience – the same group that constituted rock music's primary audience – accounted for the majority of all moviegoers. For obvious commercial reasons, Hollywood needed to incorporate rock music into its films.

Rock 'n' Roll is Here to Stay

The first rock song to appear in a movie was Bill Haley and the Comets' "Rock Around the Clock" in *The Blackboard Jungle* (1955), played over the opening credits, where it is associated with juvenile delinquency, a contemporary concern exploited by the media. In one scene, troublemaking high school students smash the math teacher's prized collection of vintage jazz 78s, at once playing on contemporary fears of juvenile delinquency and presaging the rise of rock music sweeping aside the swing music of an earlier generation. The scene was considered shocking, and Clare Booth Luce, then American ambassador to Italy, prevented the film from being shown that year at the Venice Film Festival. However, the ensuing controversy and resulting public interest not only turned the film into a box-office success but also gave what had been a minor pop hit "new life on the pop charts. By the end of the year, it had sold two million copies and provided Bill Haley with a lifetime meal ticket" (Doherty, 1988: 756). Rock 'n' roll seemed to be a lucrative fad, and exploitation filmmakers quickly jumped on the rock bandwagon.

With the exception of *The Girl Can't Help It*, early rock musicals were for the most part low-budget affairs that betrayed the film industry's condescending attitude toward rock music. Schlock producer "Jungle Sam" Katzman churned out B musicals such as *Rock Around the Clock* (1956), *Don't Knock the Rock* (1956), *Twist Around the Clock* (1961), and *Don't Knock the Twist* (1962). A little later, American International Pictures (AIP) released a string of beach musicals starring teen idols Frankie Avalon and Annette Funicello, including *Beach Party* (1963), *Muscle Beach Party* (1964), and *Beach Blanket Bingo* (1965).

Many of these movies dramatized the controversial sound of rock and the contemporary fears of teenage delinquency in their narratives. Katzman's quickies fell back on the old backstage formula, featuring several acts built around a story of a rock concert being mounted at the local high school. In *Don't Knock the Rock*, for example, rock 'n' roll has been banned because adults distrust it. Real-life disc jockey Alan Freed, an early promoter of rock 'n' roll who claimed to have invented the term, arrives to host "A Pageant of Art and Culture" by the town's teenagers, who display classic paintings and then perform a series of traditional dances, concluding with a demonstration of the Charleston. The old squares see the folly of their ways and come to accept rock 'n' roll, which is depicted as harmless fun (Plate 5). Similarly, in the non-Katzman quickie *Rock, Rock, Rock* (1956), produced by Max Rosenberg and Milton Subotsky and featuring performances by Chuck Berry, LaVern Baker, The Moonglows, The Flamingos, and Frankie Lymon and The Teen-agers, Freed agrees to broadcast his "Rock and Roll Party" TV show from the local high school gym. In the climax, Freed speaks of rock 'n' roll as a cultural melting pot, almost a microcosm of America, recalling Paul Whiteman's speech in *The King of Jazz* a quarter of a century earlier. In both films, the plot functions to close the generation gap by asserting the new form's musical continuity with previous forms of popular music. As we shall see in the following chapter, after his first few movies, in the 1960s rock superstar Elvis Presley settled into a series of amiable, predictable musicals displaying similar prosocial sentiments.

Also in the 1960s, the availability of new portable 16 mm equipment with synchronous sound capability brought about radical changes in documentary film practice and aesthetics. Many filmmakers turned their

PLATE 5 Bill Haley and His Comets having harmless fun in *Don't Knock the Rock* (Fred F. Sears, 1956; Producer: Sam Katzman).

roving, observational cameras on rock musicians, concerts, and scenes. With the new equipment, documentary filmmakers could shoot on location with relative ease, following events as they unfolded and entering into the very situations they were documenting as they happened. The first feature-length "rockumentary" was *The T.A.M.I. Show* (1964), a filmic record of a 1964 concert in Santa Monica, California, featuring The Rolling Stones, Jan and Dean, The Beach Boys, Chuck Berry, and James Brown. Documentary filmmakers now aspired to be, in Richard Leacock's famous phrase, "a fly on the wall," to capture unmediated truth on camera. During the height of what became known as the direct cinema movement in the 1960s and 1970s, choosing popular musicians as their subjects allowed documentary filmmakers access to mainstream distribution for their work at the same time as they could seek to show the real person behind the persona.

This approach was established in the first rock documentary to use the new portable equipment, the Canadian film *Lonely Boy* (1962), made by the National Film Board of Canada. About the phenomenal popularity of Canadian-born teen idol Paul Anka, *Lonely Boy* – as suggested by the

ambiguity of the film's title, itself the name of one of Anka's big hits –
manages to deconstruct even as it celebrates the image of the teen idol
(Grant, 1986: 82–5). Subsequent rock documentaries, such as Albert and
David Masyles' *What's Happening! The Beatles in the USA* (1964), D.A.
Pennebaker's *Dont Look Back* (1967) with Bob Dylan (Plate 6), and
Howard Alk's *Janis* (1974) with Janis Joplin, continued the strategy of
alternating performance sequences with more candid, backstage scenes.
The later *Madonna: Truth or Dare* (aka *In Bed with Madonna*) (1991)
deliberately plays on this convention by providing backstage scenes that
invite viewers to consider that they may be as consciously staged as the
concert performance sequences. As a subgenre, the rockumentary became
familiar enough to viewers over the next two decades that Christopher
Guest and Rob Reiner's satire *This is Spinal Tap* (1984), an account of a
fictional heavy metal band, was mistaken as real by some viewers. In fact,
Reiner's film was so popular that Spinal Tap eventually went on tour and
released a CD, *Break Like the Wind*, in 1992.

PLATE 6 Archival footage of a young Bob Dylan in the direct cinema
documentary *Dont Look Back* (D.A. Pennebaker, 1967; No producer:
Pennebaker is the "filmmaker").

By the 1970s, rock music had taken hold of the popular music scene to the extent that it would come to dominate Hollywood's big-budget glossy releases. Hollywood studios were bought by entertainment conglomerates that also owned record labels. "Fox owned Twentieth Century-Fox Records, Warner Communications Inc. (WCI) owned Warner Bros and Warner Bros Records, and MCA owned Universal Pictures and MCA Records" (Hall and Neale, 2010: 215). Already in the 1960s, Warners had acquired both Atlantic and Elektra, two extremely important independent record labels. Robert Stigwood's film musicals for Paramount, *Saturday Night Fever* (1977), considered in Chapter 6, and *Grease* (1978), followed the pattern of the 1976 (and third) version of *A Star is Born*, with 45-rpm singles and soundtrack albums released before the film. The sound tracks for *American Graffiti* and *The Big Chill* (1983) featured rock oldies that, like *Grease*, had nostalgic appeal for the baby-boomer generation and whose soundtrack LPs sold very well. In 1973, *Super Fly* became the first rock soundtrack LP to outgross its movie. Looking for further synergy between movies and rock music, Paramount promoted *Flashdance* (1983) on MTV, which began broadcasting just two years earlier, in 1981. The video of Michael Sembello's "Maniac" was released to the channel a month before the opening of the film, "which enabled it to play a key role in the cross-promotion of the film, album and single" (Hall and Neale, 2010). Further, the musical sequences were designed with a "modular" approach that allowed them to be easily lifted from the film and adapted to the music video format (Hall and Neale, 2010).

Music Video

Although music videos as we understand them today were not a significant presence in the cultural landscape until the early 1980s, when MTV went on the air, there are a number of antecedents to this postmodern form.

Short 16 mm films known as "soundies" were produced during the war years. A rudimentary form of music video, soundies were made for coin-operated rear projection machines called Panorams, located in public places such as nightclubs, bars, and restaurants. They featured all musical styles, from Irish folksongs to country music to big band swing, and many jazz musicians appeared in them, including Stan Kenton, Count Basie, Duke Ellington, and Nat King Cole. The Panoram machines were a precursor to and eventually replaced by the jukebox, which would become pervasive in the postwar era and be indelibly associated with the new music of rock 'n' roll.

In the 1960s and 1970s, as cross-promotional strategies intensified, *Butch Cassidy and the Sundance Kid* (1969), a buddy-buddy western starring Paul Newman and Robert Redford, included a non-diegetic musical interlude featuring B.J. Thomas singing his charted hit version of Burt Bacharach and Hal David's "Raindrops Keep Falling on My Head" while Newman, Redford, and Katharine Ross cavort on a bicycle. The sequence was entirely irrelevant to the film's narrative, but it was a catchy tune and became a pop hit for Thomas. The sequence is a perfect example of what Roger Ebert has called the "semi-obligatory musical interlude" or "Semi-OLI": "a scene in which soft focus and slow motion are used while a would-be hit song is performed on the sound track and the lovers run through a pastoral setting." This form, which Ebert notes was "[c]ommon from the mid-1960s to the mid-1970s," was replaced in the 1980s with "the Semi-Obligatory Music Video," which he defines as a "[t]hree-minute sequence within otherwise ordinary narrative structure, in which a song is played at top volume while movie characters experience spasms of hyperkinetic behavior and stick their faces into the camera lens" (Ebert n.d.).

Several film musicals employed a more flashy, kinetic visual style, very different from the style associated with Berkeley, Astaire, or Kelly, that aesthetically matched the power of the rock music featured on the sound track. Ken Russell's *Tommy* (1975), adapted from the rock opera by The Who, and Alan Parker's *Pink Floyd: The Wall* (1982) featured rapid editing and startling imagery that mirrored – and, in the case of Russell's film, anticipated – the style of music videos (Plate 7). Russell, a British filmmaker, earlier made a series of flashy biopics about artists, particularly classical musicians, including *Elgar* (1962), *Bartok* (1964), *The Music Lovers* (1970, Tchaikovsky), and *Mahler* (1974), that hinted at this developing style. His screen version of Sandy Wilson's parodic homage to the classic Warner Bros musicals, *The Boy Friend* (1971), signaled his distance from the genre's traditions. In the outlandish *Lisztomania* (1975), composer Franz Liszt (played by Roger Daltrey, vocalist of The Who) is shown as a rock star of his era playing his "big hit," "Chopsticks," in concert for an audience of appreciative groupies.

The imagery of Russell's biopics is frequently hyperbolic and surreal, such as the scene of Ann-Margret writhing in mountains of baked beans, detergent foam, and chocolate in *Tommy* or Daltrey's Liszt blasting off in a penis-shaped rocket. Russell also often relies on striking pictorial effects in individual images apart from their narrative context. Musical biopics from *The Great Ziegfeld* (1936) and *Night and Day* (1946, starring Cary Grant as Cole Porter), to *The Buddy Holly Story* (1978), *What's Love Got to Do with*

PLATE 7 Guitarist Eric Clapton as a priest leading his flock of fans in Ken Russell's adaptation of The Who's rock opera *Tommy* (Ken Russell, 1975; Producer: Robert Stigwood).

It? (1993, about R&B singer Tina Turner), and *Ray* (2004, about Ray Charles, the "genius of soul"), present chronological accounts of their subject's life (however factual or melodramatized they may be), but Russell's biopics construct more complex cinematic biographies in which the excessive imagery functions to express not only the facts of the artist's life but also and simultaneously the artist's own romantic opinion of himself as well as the filmmaker's view of him (Gomez, 1976: 35).

The "psychedelic" style of Russell's films influenced the postmode style of music videos that emerged shortly thereafter. Many critics hav discussed music videos, in their reliance on pastiche, intertextuality, and pictorial effects, as an essential postmodern form. E. Ann Kaplan, one of the first scholars to discuss them, argues, further, that the surface visual style of music videos, considered in the context of their televisual flow, addresses the viewer as a postmodern consumer: "MTV functions like one continuous ad in that nearly all of its short segments are indeed ads of one kind or another. It is for this reason that MTV, more than any other television, may be said to be about consumption" (Kaplan, 1987: 12). Not coincidentally, consumption is precisely the target of the Ann-Margret scene in *Tommy*.

The dynamic visual style associated with music videos seems a suitable accompaniment for the more frenetic types of contemporary dance that, with the innovations of Michael Jackson, have replaced the older styles of tap, ballroom, and ballet dancing represented by Astaire and Kelly. Certainly by the time of *Dirty Dancing* (1987), dancing "cheek to cheek" means something entirely different than when Astaire sang it to Rogers in *Top Hat*. Whereas the dancers in earlier musicals are presented in long takes and full shots that displayed their performances in real time, dance numbers in musicals such as *Flashdance, Moulin Rouge!, Chicago* (2002), and *Burlesque* (2010) tended to be built from numerous short shots combined with dizzy montage effects and peripatetic camera movement. *Flashdance*, which stars Jennifer Beale as an improbable dancer and steel welder, thus was able to substitute a body double for the dance sequences, and to build her gymnastic steps from the dancing of two other performers as well. *Chicago*, in case viewers might suspect trickery because of its editing, includes a note in the end credits that explicitly states that all the actors, including normally dramatic performers such as Richard Gere, actually did their own singing and dancing.

New Steps

In Stanley Kubrick's *A Clockwork Orange* (1971), a group of teenage thugs invade the home of a defenseless couple, and their leader, Alex (Malcolm McDowell), rapes and beats the wife while dancing and singing "Singin' in the Rain." This shocking scene in Kubrick's futuristic nightmare anticipates the darker turn that some musicals have taken in more recent years. The 1970s was a period of significant changes in genre filmmaking as the studio system crumbled, the Production Code was replaced by a ratings system, and a new generation of directors conscious of film history emerged (Cawelti, 2003). As discussed in the analysis of Brian De Palma's *Phantom of the Paradise* (1974) in Chapter 8, younger filmmakers revisited Hollywood's classic genres, including the musical. Even as the classic film musical was being enshrined in the two *That's Entertainment!* compilations, parodies such as Russell's *The Boy Friend* and *Movie Movie* (1978) – directed by none other than Stanley Donen, co-director with Gene Kelly of *Singin' in the Rain* and *It's Always Fair Weather* and director of *Funny Face* (1957), *The Pajama Game* (1957), and *Damn Yankees!* (1958) – were poking fun at the genre's classic conventions. Film musicals such as the psychedelic western *Zachariah* (1971), the sci-fi parody *The Rocky Horror Picture Show* (1975) (Plate 8), *The First Nudie Musical* (1976), *Saturday Night Fever, Hair* (1979), and *Pennies from Heaven* in different ways undermined the genre's stylistic and thematic conventions. Meanwhile, Robert Altman's *Nashville* (1975) and Martin Scorsese's *New York, New York* (1977) both invoked the genre's traditions but with a more dystopian vision.

All That Jazz (1979), which was nominated for nine Academy Awards and won four, is representative of the new postmodern musical. A semi-autobiographical musical by writer/actor/choreographer/editor/director

PLATE 8 The cult classic *The Rocky Horror Picture Show* (Jim Sharman, 1975) was one of several film musicals in the 1970s that subverted the genre's conventions (Producers: Lou Adler, John Goldstone, Michael White).

Bob Fosse, *All That Jazz* is a postmodern pastiche of pop music, right from its opening audition montage edited to George Benson's version of "On Broadway," and is more cynical of the genre's classic myths (see Chapter 2). Fosse, who developed a distinctive angular style of dance with sexual overtones as the choreographer for several hit Broadway musicals, including *The Pajama Game* and *Damn Yankees!*, moved to film directing with the musical *Sweet Charity* (1969), starring Shirley MacLaine, an adaptation of the Broadway musical he had directed and choreographed based on Federico Fellini's *Le Notti di Cabiria* (1957). His second film, *Cabaret* (1972), another musical, won eight Academy Awards, including Best Director, beating out Francis Ford Coppola for *The Godfather*.

All That Jazz was inspired by Fosse's frantic effort to edit his film *Lenny* (1974), a non-musical biopic about controversial comedian Lenny Bruce, while creating his 1975 Broadway musical, *Chicago*. In *All That Jazz*, musical director Joe Gideon (Roy Scheider), like Julian Marsh in *42nd Street*, has a bad heart. But that is where the similarities between the two films end. Gideon is a womanizing cad addicted to amphetamines to help him with his busy work schedule; he works the cast to the bone not to create a show for the common good, but to satisfy his own obsession with artistic perfection. Popping his pills each morning as he prepares for work, he says "It's showtime" as he looks at his reflection in the mirror, the phrase coming to mean putting on a game face rather than revealing one's authentic self. And instead of offering a choreographed vision of romance and grace frozen in time, as in the Astaire–Rogers films, *All That Jazz* emphasizes impermanence and mortality. After Gideon suffers a heart attack, his bypass surgery is intercut with the producers' discussion about whether it would be better financially to cancel the show or replace Gideon. Toward the end of the film, after Gideon accepts the fact that he is dying, a production number featuring the Everly Brothers' 1957 hit "Bye Bye Love" is redone as "Bye Bye Life," with the dancers wearing body suits with the circulatory system imprinted on them. *All That Jazz* explicitly underscores its distance from generic tradition when Gideon, in an extreme high-angle shot, rendering him puny as he prowls the dank bowels of the hospital in despair, suddenly looks up at the camera and ironically asks the audience, "Don't you like musical comedy?"

Like *All That Jazz*, the more romantic *Moulin Rouge!*, directed, produced, and co-written by Australian filmmaker Baz Luhrmann, who also wrote and directed the earlier *Strictly Ballroom* (1992), ends with death as well. Set in Paris at the turn of the twentieth century, its story involves a young English writer, Christian (Ewan MacGregor), and a cabaret performer and courtesan, Satine (Nicole Kidman); they fall in love, as in so many musicals, despite numerous obstacles; but in the end, as the lovers finish their song to a standing ovation from the audience, instead of dancing off happily ever after, Satine expires from a fatal illness. Also like *All That Jazz*, *Moulin Rouge!* features a pastiche of contemporary popular music styles and tunes, in this case presenting them in an obviously anachronistic context. In the notes for the Special Edition DVD of the film, Luhrmann writes that the "whole stylistic premise has been to decode what the Moulin Rouge was to the audiences of 1899 and express that same thrill and excitement in a way to which contemporary movie-goers can relate." With a vertiginous editing style like music videos featuring a peripatetic camera, rapid editing, and bold compositions, the songs in the film include Patti LaBelle's "Lady Marmalade," Madonna's "Like a Virgin" (sung, surprisingly, by male actor Jim Broadbent) and "Material Girl," Elton John's "Your Song," Nirvana's "Smells Like Teen Spirit," Sting and The Police's "Roxanne," and the title song from *The Sound of Music* (1965).

In the 1970s, *Willie Wonka and the Chocolate Factory* (1971), *Bedknobs and Broomsticks* (1971), and *Bugsy Malone* (1976), a musical gangster film with a cast of children including Jodie Foster, Scott Baio, and Michael Jackson, pointed the way beyond the juvenilization of the genre to its infantilization with musicals for children. Since the 1980s the Disney studio has dominated the field, with a steady flow of animated musicals including *The Little Mermaid* (1989), *Beauty and the Beast* (1991), *Aladdin* (1992), *The Lion King* (1994), and *Pocahontas* (1995). Disney's earlier avant-garde animated feature *Fantasia* (1940) had a wall-to-wall sound track of classical music, and the studio's animated features for children such as *Cinderella* (1950) and *Peter Pan* (1953) had contained several songs. The studio's newer animated musicals offered encouraging messages of empowerment for children while providing humorous cultural references for parents, who would, after all, be the ones taking their children and paying for the movie at the box office. *The Little Mermaid*, an adaptation of a Hans Christian Andersen fairy tale featuring a lush Tin Pan Alley score by Howard Ashman and Allan Menken, earned over $100 million in its theatrical release alone, in addition to its substantial sales on home video. The film also won Oscars for Best Song ("Under the Sea") and Best Original Score and generated a Grammy-winning soundtrack CD and animated TV series. Later, "A Whole New World" from *Aladdin* received the Academy Award for Best Song, as did "Colors of the Wind" from *Pocahontas*. Disney also struck gold with its extraordinary popular live-action musical series for its own channel, *Hannah Montana* (2006–10, feature film 2009), starring Miley Cyrus, as well as, beginning in 2006, the first of four *High School Musical* films.

All in all, there is no question that there have been fewer film musicals made in the last few decades. And if some, like *Fame* (1980), *Little Shop of Horrors* (1986), with music by Ashman and Menken, and *High School Musical* (2006), have been popular, others, such as *Nine* (2009) and *Burlesque*, starring Cher and Christina Aguilera, bombed at the box office. On the big screen, musicals have a difficult time competing with the more aggressively kinetic genres of action and adventure which have so dominated North American movie screens of late. However, television has stepped in to fill the gap. On TV in the 1950s *Ted Mack's Original Amateur Hour* (1948–54) and *Arthur Godfrey's Talent Scouts* (1946–56), both of which began on radio, showcased aspiring entertainers (Pat Boone and Gladys Knight were among those who appeared on the former, Tony Bennett and Patsy Cline on the latter). In recent years, though, this type of show has become more prominent as part of the wider popularity of "reality TV," as seen on very popular shows such as *Dancing with the Stars* (2005–), *So You Think You Can Dance* (2005–), *American Idol* (2002–), and *America's Got Talent* (2006–). Other countries have their versions of some of these shows as well. The shows provide training opportunities for new talent to develop and come to the public's attention.

In the past, the few musical television series that were broadcast, such as *That's Life* (1968–9), *Dirty Dancing* (1988–9), and *Cop Rock* (1990), met with limited success (Hillier and Pye, 2011: 13). More recently, however, the hit series *Glee* (2009–) shows the continuing appeal of musical entertainment, as does the phenomenon of flashmob videos going viral. The rise to star magnitude of Justin Bieber similarly demonstrates the power of the internet to shape contemporary popular music. With the increasing use of social media and websites such as YouTube, the film musical may continue to move away from the narrative integration that characterized its golden age. At the same time, these changes may bring us closer to the musical's utopian vision because now we all have equal access to the technology to create and publicly screen movies of ourselves singing and dancing if we so choose.

CHAPTER 2

CRITICAL OVERVIEW

Just as film musicals have appealed to audiences since their beginning, so has the genre attracted the attention of many critics and scholars. Much of this critical and theoretical work has focused on individual films, such as *42nd Street* (1933), *Meet Me in St Louis* (1944), and *Showboat* (1951), and specific directors acknowledged as auteurs who have contributed substantially to the genre, such as Busby Berkeley and Vincente Minnelli. Early books on the film musical were historical overviews ranging from generously illustrated coffee-table volumes to rigorously researched works. Theoretical work about the genre began to appear in the 1970s. Generally writers have tended to understand trends and cycles of the genre as reflective of the cultural zeitgeist at the time of their making. Thus Warner Bros' musicals of the 1930s have been interpreted as a response to the conditions of the Great Depression (e.g., Roth, 1980), and the MGM musicals of the 1950s, as reflecting the erosion of American triumphalism during the Cold War (e.g., M. Wood, 1975). In recent years, critics have approached musicals in terms of identity politics, considering how musicals represent class, race, gender, and sexuality.

No brief overview can hope to acknowledge all of the disparate work that has been done on the film musical. Accordingly, this chapter organizes discussion around several themes and theoretical ideas that have emerged as the most common and most productive for discussing and understanding

The Hollywood Film Musical, First Edition. Barry Keith Grant.
© 2012 Barry Keith Grant. Published 2012 by Blackwell Publishing Ltd.

the genre. These themes are taken up to varying degree in the close readings that follow.

Apparatus

The term "apparatus" in film and cultural studies is used in two senses. First, it refers to the physical equipment and technology that allow for mass duplication of an original in the media for dissemination to a wide public. Second, it points to the related aesthetic, economic, and ideological structures and contexts within which that medium exists. The "music industry" and the "film industry" are capitalist systems of production and distribution of goods for profit, a chain of economic structures including the talent, studios, manufacturers, retailers, and consumers. Both industries are dependent upon technology at every level.

It is one of the foundational premises of film studies that the image is a representation and as such is different from the thing it is an image of, and that it is possible for films and filmmakers to exploit this difference through stylistic means for thematic purposes. Although it is not as frequently noted, the same idea applies to recorded music – that is, music as mediated through the recording apparatus. As Alan Williams observes, because of the mediating function of recording, recorded sound is different from the original sound or "sonic event" produced by musicians. Thus recording is itself a "signifying practice" with sonic manipulations analogous to those of image recording: edits, dissolves, and superimpositions, for example (Williams, 1980: 51, 60). Considering the difference between music and the recording of it, philosopher Evan Eisenberg refers to the latter as the art of "phonography" – the art of recorded music as distinct from music. He refers to such otherwise disparate artists as Edgar Varèse, Glenn Gould, Duke Ellington, Thelonious Monk, Miles Davis, Frank Zappa, Phil Spector, and The Beatles as the great phonographers who "built" records as layered sound objects. For Eisenberg, Enrico Caruso and Louis Armstrong were "icons of phonography," disembodied voices that were at one time omnipresent and distinctly recognizable by the entire culture, like visual icons (Eisenberg, 1987: 105, 127).

The history of the blues provides a striking example both of the extent to which the apparatus affects the art and of the inextricable relationship between aesthetics and technology in the recording industry. The blues form originally had two strains, the narrative and the lyrical. As the terms suggest, the former told stories in a string of verses, the latter evoked moods. But because the recording time of 78 rpm records were only three to four minutes in length, the strain of narrative blues all but died out after the 1920s because they had too many verses to fit onto a record. Thus the limitations of the technology determined the content of the repertoire, which in turn shaped the tradition (Charters, 1979: 32).

The cinematic apparatus figures just as prominently in the case of the film musical. Most obviously, synchronized sound technology was a prerequisite for the existence of the genre. Further, as Williams points out, "[t]he director and sound recording engineer have done the work of our perception, negotiating the real world for us. . . . [I]n sound recording, as in image recording, the apparatus performs a significant perceptual work *for us* – isolating, intensifying, analyzing sonic and visual material. It gives us an implied physical perspective on image and sound source" (Williams, 1989: 58). Thus, just as in film there is a "spectating subject," so with recorded music there is a "listening subject."

The idea of the sound track as engineered, as constructed, has important implications for the analysis of film musicals, particularly regarding the common practice of dubbing, in which the voice of an unseen performer substitutes for that of the person onscreen. In *West Side Story* (1961), for example (discussed in greater detail in Chapter 6), romantic leads Richard Beymer (Tony) and Natalie Wood (Maria) attempted to do their own singing for the film, but the music supervisors Saul Chaplin and Johnny Green considered their voices too rough for the image they were seeking, so the actors were overdubbed with the voices of other singers (Jimmy Bryant and Marni Nixon, respectively). Nixon sang the soprano parts of Maria's songs, and Wood the lower parts, similar to the blending of Nixon's voice with Marilyn Monroe's for "Diamonds are a Girl's Best Friend" in *Gentlemen Prefer Blondes* (1953). Similarly, the voice of Tucker Smith, who plays Ice, one of the Jets, and who sings "Cool," was dubbed by Russ Tamblyn, who plays Riff, although Smith's own voice is heard on the novelty number "Gee, Officer Krupke," and the voice of Rita Moreno (Anita) was dubbed by Betty Wand for "A Boy Like That," but Moreno's own voice is used in "America." French cultural theorist Roland Barthes identifies what he calls "the 'grain' of the voice" as "the body in the voice as it sings, the hand as it writes, the limb as it performs" (Barthes, 1977: 188). *West Side Story* crafts a deliberate visual and aural "grain" for its protagonists to evoke a youthful romanticism with which viewers can readily identify, heightening the emotional power of its tragic climax.

Singin' in the Rain (1952) offers a more complex example of how dubbing may relate to the film's meaning. Set during Hollywood's transition to sound in the late 1920s, this musical offers a comic look at the difficulties filmmakers experienced with the new sound equipment. In the plot, Lina Lamont (Jean Hagen), a silent film star based partially on real-life actress Norma Talmadge, has an awful voice and so her sound film debut is dubbed by Kathy Seldon (Debbie Reynolds). Ironically, Reynolds was herself dubbed in "Would You?" and "You are My Lucky Star" by Betty Noyes, who was uncredited. And when Kathy is supposedly dubbing Lina's voice in the reprise of "Singin' in the Rain" at the end, Hagen dubbed Reynolds' speaking voice. Thus the film provides the same kind of aural manipulations that it mocks in the plot, and from this perspective may be seen as a contradictory text.

Beyond individual films, one might read the genre's history as a dialectic between the realist and expressionist tendencies of cinema. As discussed in the previous chapter, the genre has at times preferred the long take and moving camera during production numbers, displaying the action in real time in order to preserve a sense of the performance's wholeness. By contrast, production numbers in Busby Berkeley's films and more recent musicals such as *Flashdance* (1983), *Moulin Rouge!* (2001), and *Chicago* (2002) (Plate 9) tend to be built from numerous short shots combined with dizzying montage effects and peripatetic camera movement. Regardless of a particular musical's style, however, performances in film inevitably raise questions, despite their efforts to seem spontaneous (see following section). How many takes were required for Astaire to dance while playing a drum kit in *A Damsel in Distress* (1937)? Did Donald O'Connor really run up the wall and do a flip off it in *Singin' in the Rain* (1952)? Is Richard Gere, normally a dramatic actor, really dancing in *Chicago*?

Community and Utopia

All genre movies deal in one way or another with reconciling individual and group values. This is a conflict that we constantly negotiate, psychologically and socially, as part of life, but for which there is no ultimate answer. For this reason, genre movies appeal to us as cultural ritual, replaying the same narratives with slight variations time and again, and offering us comfortable narrative resolutions for irresolvable questions. Much genre criticism, informed by the structuralist theories of anthropologist Claude Lévi-Strauss, sees genres as addressing cultural binaries that in reality are irreconcilable; their narrative closure provides audiences with satisfying resolutions despite — indeed, because of — their conventionality and similarity. As subsequent chapters demonstrate, the film musical specifically is concerned with such thematic oppositions as

PLATE 9 Catherine Zeta-Jones as Velma Kelly in the stylish *Chicago* (Rob Marshall, 2002; Producer: Martin Richards).

"order/liberty" and "work/entertainment" (Altman, 1987: 27), although these terms may be defined differently from film to film.

For genre theorist Thomas Schatz, "[a]ll genre films treat some form of threat – violent or otherwise – to the social order," although different genres approach this threat in different ways (Schatz, 1981: 26). The gangster, the monster, and the heroine of screwball comedy all threaten normative society, and, as we shall see, the same can be said for a variety of characters and the meanings they embody in the film musical. The characters in musicals may not signify crime and anarchy like the gangster, corruption and violence like the gunfighter in the western, or bodily violation and death like the monsters of horror, but they nevertheless do embody values that pose challenges to the harmonious functioning of society. The word "harmonious" is deliberate here, because in film musicals these conflicts are of course worked out in terms of the music and singing and dancing.

Schatz distinguishes between what he calls genres of "determinate" and "indeterminate" space. The former involve a physical conflict in a conventionalized arena (Main Street at high noon in the western, the city's mean streets in the gangster film) and address social integration, with the physical threat to society forcefully eradicated. By contrast, the genres of indeterminate space – musical, screwball comedy, melodrama – are concerned more with social order, coding the conflict within the tribulations of a heterosexual relationship. These genres frequently "rely upon a progression from romantic antagonism to eventual embrace. The kiss or embrace signals the integration of the couple into the larger cultural community" (Schatz, 1981: 27–9). Gender construction is central to the ideological work of movies generally, but particularly central to the film musical (Babington and Evans, 1985). In musicals such as *Top Hat* (1935) and *The Pirate* (1948), discussed in detail in Chapters 4 and 5, respectively, these "tribulations" involve the "taming" of male sexual energy and its harnessing to the model of the heterosexual, monogamous couple. The establishment of the couple maintains the status quo and in its conventional "happily ever after" ending suggests its ideological correctness. The narrative closure of *Seven Brides for Seven Brothers* (1954) only multiplies the outcome of many other film musicals (Plate 10).

Beyond the traditional couple, the wider social context is addressed by the importance of community in the film musical. In the genre's musical numbers, lead performers often sing and dance in the company of other people, often represented in the form of a diegetic audience, and with other people, most commonly with supporting players or a larger chorus, either

PLATE 10 All the couples kiss in *Seven Brides for Seven Brothers* (Stanley Donen, 1954; Producer: Jack Cummings).

singing or dancing along. In *The Band Wagon* (1953), Fred Astaire's solitary singing of "I'll Go My Way by Myself" is effectively countered by the surprise party mounted by his supportive cast, the moment articulating the genre's typical social thrust. Within the film musical's plot, community may be presented in a variety of ways, from the cast of the show-within-the-film in *The Band Wagon* to street gangs in lower Manhattan in *West Side Story* and women prison inmates in *Chicago*, but all groups in musicals that sing and dance together inevitably express a sense of communal solidarity in their shared participation in performance. Whether this sense of community is defined as, for example, an idealized folk culture in the Freed Unit musicals (Feuer, 1993) or as American patriotism during World War II (Woll, 1983), the film musical overwhelmingly tends toward a vision of social integration.

Jane Feuer claims that Hollywood musicals mask their carefully constructed origins, created by many workers within an industrial system, by making musical performance seem spontaneous within the narrative rather than carefully choreographed. As she puts it, they "cancel engineering (a characteristic of mass production) by substituting *bricolage* (a characteristic of folk production)" (Feuer, 1993: 5). Performers "tinker" with things in their dance numbers as if they were found objects rather than props placed on a set (Feuer, 1993: 3–5). Among countless examples one might cite Fred Astaire's dance in the boiler room in *Shall We Dance* (1937) and the "Moses Supposes" number in *Singin' in the Rain*, in which Gene Kelly and Donald O'Connor bury their elocution teacher in various objects in his office.

According to Feuer, "the creation of folk relations in the films cancels the mass entertainment substance of the films. The Hollywood musical becomes a mass art which aspires to the condition of a folk art, produced and consumed by the same integrated community" (Feuer, 1993: 3). Part of this ideological strategy involves the integration of highbrow and lowbrow art into middlebrow entertainment, of which the film musical itself is an example. In *The Band Wagon*, for instance, the flamboyant impresario Jeffrey Cordova (Jack Buchanan) turns the show folks' musical comedy into an overblown production of *Faust*, which the film mocks as pretentious and depicts as a disaster on opening night. The reversion of the show to a musical comedy brings success and a resolution of the conflict between the ballet dancer Gabrielle Gerard (Cyd Charisse) and the tap dancer Tony Hunter (Astaire) and the respective values of high and popular art that they represent. The wave of quickie rock musicals in the mid-1950s, discussed in the previous chapter, offer other examples of the same ideological impulse.

It may be true, as William Pechter notes, that the Italian neorealist filmmakers "have demonstrated that everyone is a potential film actor, but no one has gone very far with the democratic proposition that anyone can sing or dance" (Pechter, 1982: 80). On a literal level, a musical like Peter Bogdanovich's *At Long Last Love* (1975), which deliberately cast non-singers Burt Reynolds and Cybil Shepard in starring roles, would seem to support Pechter's observation. Yet for Feuer and others, the film musical erases the idea of any distinction between aristocrat and commoner, instead depicting a democratic show business community. As discussed in Chapter 3, the Warner Bros musicals of the early 1930s such as *Gold Diggers of 1933* (1933) and *42nd Street*, for example, erase class distinctions, among other differences, by reconciling the snobbish Boston elite with New York working girls. Ultimately the film musical dissolves even political differences. In 1957, *Silk Stockings* managed to reduce the contemporary political tensions of the Cold War to the genre's typical play of heterosexual seduction and conquest. "Music will dissolve the Iron Curtain," asserts the confident, red-blooded American Steve Canfield (Astaire) as he sets out to woo Ninotchka Yoschenko (Charisse), the cold-blooded commissar, and indeed he succeeds with the help of American entertainment.

Movie musicals thus offer a social utopia, but they also depict a utopian state of plenitude and fulfillment. As suggested at the outset, in movie musicals, characters are able to satisfy their desire or at least to feel better by dancing or singing. This is true whether they are feeling up or down, whether they are alone or in public. And when others join in, it is as if the entire world has become attuned to their feelings. In so doing, musicals depict an ideal integration of mental and physical life, of mind and body, where intangible feeling is given form as concrete yet gracious physical action. This is not a social utopia so much as "the feelings" that utopia embodies. For Richard Dyer, the musical "presents, head-on, as it were, what utopia would feel like rather than how it would be organized" (Dyer, 1980: 177). The latter is more the concern of science fiction. This, for Dyer, is the ideological function of all musical entertainment, including the film musical. In his influential discussion of entertainment, he says that musicals "work" as escapist entertainment because of their ability to present complex and unpleasant feelings in simple, direct, and vivid ways (Dyer, 1980: 182).

Romance, Sexuality, and Gender

The importance of romance and the construction of the couple in the film musical inevitably raises questions about the genre's representation of gender and sexuality. The musical's concern with articulating a sense of community as well as defining the parameters of sexual desire are, of course, related, as the regulation of sexuality is crucial to the maintenance of social order. As already noted, this theme is articulated with mythic repetition in the series of musicals starring Fred Astaire and Ginger Rogers in the 1930s, as well as in many later musicals with Gene Kelly, but also informs numerous other movies in the genre. The romantic subplot is central to classic Hollywood cinema generally (Bordwell *et al.*, 1985: 16), but is especially pronounced in the musical. Rick Altman observes that many musicals share a dual focus of a narrative conflict that is mirrored by a romantic subplot (Altman, 1987: 16ff.). Typically, the romantic plot in the film musical involves a developing attraction between the protagonists that is complicated by a misunderstanding that in turn is eventually resolved with the couple getting together in marriage or its promise.

Just as the primary subject of popular music is love, so the great theme of the film musical, like Shakespearean comedy, is romance, which it tends to depict according to the honeyed clichés of pop music. Typically, love in the musical, from *Flying Down to Rio* (1933) to *Moulin Rouge!* is of the wonderful "some-enchanted-evening" variety, where lovers are depicted as destined for each other, and after an inevitable series of delays and obstacles, they get together and presumably live happily ever after. In *An American in Paris* (1951), the Gene Kelly character Jerry is inexplicably blind to the obvious charms of Nina Foch but irredeemably smitten with Leslie Caron upon his first view of her. The connection between music and romance is hardly surprising, given western culture's understanding of music as abstract and without tangible properties, hence the most "pure" of the arts, transcendent, capable of speaking directly to the emotions or the soul (see Green, 1988). Typically, the narrative conflict in a musical is resolved when the couple's differences are reconciled, generally through the mediating power of musical performance, resulting in the lovers' union. Before we know it, the leading players are smoothly in step. When coded as dance, the rituals of courtship come to seem graceful rather than, as they so often are in the real world, ungainly and awkward.

At the same time, the film musical exploits the metaphorical connections between dance and sex. When a couple dance well, often "spontaneously" – as they conventionally seem to do in musicals – their bodies move in graceful harmony, their synchronization a sign of their spiritual and physical union. This state is, of course, also the ideal experience not only of being in love but of making love, and so this metaphorical meaning of dance has been common in popular culture since the 1920s. In film, musical performance provides a conventionalized way of addressing issues of sex indirectly, in a manner suitable to both audiences and the demands of the Production Code, the system of self-regulation instituted by the Hollywood studios in the 1930s. Filmmakers could show couples dancing together, performing for the camera, rather than having to show them chastely kissing followed by the conventional fadeout to suggest lovemaking. One of the satisfactions provided by the film musical genre is that it can acknowledge and express a sense of our desire (in the musical numbers) while at the same time safely containing it socially (in the narrative). If the western hero rides off into the sunset and the detective hero walks alone down those mean streets, in the film musical, characters are almost always united in the end in heterosexual partnership. The transformation of (masculine) desire into romance tames any potential threat to the larger social community.

The movie career of rock superstar Elvis Presley is commonly regarded as exemplifying the mainstreaming of masculine sexual energy in the film musical. In his first films, *Loving You* (1956), *Jailhouse Rock* (1957), and *King Creole* (1958), Presley played fiery, rebellious characters that invoked his real-life persona; but in time Presley was transformed into a nice all-American boy in a series of largely indistinguishable and innocuous musicals with tepid pop music. In the early *Loving You*, Presley's character, Deke Rivers, surprises everyone with his sexual charisma when he sings. The movie's conventional climactic national TV broadcast becomes a forum for deciding whether Presley "should be allowed to sing anywhere he pleases." Reaction to his performance is likened to that at the premiere of Stravinsky's *Rite of Spring*, but in the end everyone comes to appreciate his style and he is paired off with the wholesome younger woman played by Dolores Hart. In *G.I. Blues* (1960), Elvis plays a good young man who babysits and sings to puppets, and in *Blue Hawaii* (1961) he enjoys surfing and hanging out with his girlfriend (Plate 11). By the time of *Frankie and Johnny* (1966), his distinctive, sexually charged movements – amply on display in earlier films in sequences such as the title number of *Jailhouse Rock*, for which Presley created his own choreography – have been almost completely constrained, his musical numbers placed in such unlikely contexts as a conventional marching band. In his penultimate film, *Change of Habit* (1969), Presley is cast as a crusading ghetto doctor, socially acceptable enough that Mary Tyler Moore can contemplate leaving the convent for a secular marriage with him without alienating the movie audience. His subsequent triumph in Las Vegas and the successful marketing of a variety of Elvis merchandise reduced Presley's image to the nostalgically sentimentalized figure of Henry Winkler's Fonzie on the television sitcom *Happy Days* (1974–84) and the character of Danny Zuko (John Travolta) in *Grease* (1978).

In addition to the representations onscreen, some film scholars have considered the visual style of movie musicals from the perspective of sexuality and gender. For example, feminist critics have shown how Berkeley's choreography makes women the objects of erotic voyeurism and firmly endorses patriarchal values. The famous sequence from *The Gang's All Here* (1943), featuring Carmen Miranda as "The Lady in the Tutti-Frutti Hat" along with a line of chorus girls waving giant bananas, underscores the Freudian and sexual symbolism in Berkeley's work. As discussed in Chapter 3, *Gold Diggers of 1933* opens with the chorines singing "We're in the Money" clad in nothing but large coins – a perfect image of the exchange value of women within patriarchal culture. For Lucy Fischer, "Berkeley's plastic abstractions present us with... a vision of female stereotypes in their purest, most distillate form.... It tends, in fact, to literalize the stereotype of the male director as potent Svengali who transforms the dull but malleable female form into an alluring screen presence" (Fischer, 1980: 76).

PLATE 11 Elvis Presley cuts a clean rug in *Blue Hawaii* (Norman Taurug, 1961; Producer: Hal B. Wallis).

Yet, as Steve Neale notes, the musical is "the only genre in which the male body has been unashamedly put on display in mainstream cinema in any consistent way" (Neale, 1993: 18). Although Neale seems to regard this display as "feminizing" the male performer, Steven Cohan, picking up on his observation, explores Fred Astaire's image in his musicals and concludes that it is more accurate to describe the situation as constructing both masculinity and femininity in the film musical from theatricalized performances of gender (Cohan, 1993: 48). While not denying that the images of women are eroticized for a male viewer, constructed for their "to-be-looked-at-ness" according to Laura Mulvey (1989: 19), Cohan argues that "song-and-dance men" in musicals are treated similarly. Astaire's roles collectively employ tropes associated with the "feminine" (narcissism, exhibitionism, masquerade) but at the same time exhibit "a musical persona whose energy choreographs a libidinal force that revises conventional masculinity" (Cohan, 1993: 63–4).

Race

The history of American popular music mirrors the convoluted and unfortunate history of race relations in the United States, particularly regarding African Americans, who have contributed so much to American musical entertainment. Like American society, popular music was at one time largely segregated. Consider the irony of the fact that black customers were not admitted to the Cotton Club, the famous Harlem nightclub where black bands such as Duke Ellington's regularly played. Major record companies like Columbia produced separate series of black blues and jazz, which would be marketed as "race music" or with euphemisms such as a "sepia" catalogue. In the realm of popular music, as elsewhere, black Americans were exploited and oppressed.

The popular practice of cover versions in the 1950s would not have been possible without such institutionalized segregation. Today, the term refers merely to a new version of a song originally recorded by someone else; but in the 1950s it was a deliberate practice whereby major labels had white artists record rhythm 'n' blues songs by black artists originally released on smaller independent labels, toning down the black sound for a wider (that is, white) audience. Such covering of black music depended upon the segregation of the pop and r&b charts. Also, the country's main radio stations avoided playing r&b, while the smaller stations that catered to black audiences, with their lower wattage and range, were largely unable to penetrate the wider market. As a result, many white listeners, particularly in rural areas, were completely unaware of the originals and so bought the cover versions, turning them into mainstream hits while the original records never broke out of smaller regional markets. The r&b labels themselves often conspired in the practice, alerting the majors to potential cover tunes, for whatever profit these smaller labels might lose from the sale of their own records could be increased by royalties from larger sales in the mainstream white market. Of course, the artists themselves lost out on the royalties, as the copyrights would be controlled by the labels for which they recorded. The most prolific white cover artist in the 1950s was Pat Boone, a squeaky-clean youth in white buckskin shoes who covered Fats Domino's "Ain't That a Shame," Little Richard's "Tutti Frutti," Roy Brown's "Good Rockin' Tonight," and The Flamingos' "I'll Be Home," all for the mainstream Dot label. Nor was such cultural theft confined to music. For Michael Rogin, "just as *The Jazz Singer* appropriated African American music, so *Singin' in the Rain* steals African American dance" (Rogin, 1996: 206).

In movies, black artists were similarly segregated. The phenomenon of musicals from major studios featuring all-black casts such as *Hallelujah* (1929), *Cabin in the Sky* (1943) (Plate 12), and *Carmen Jones* (1954) is the most obvious expression of this racial apartheid. *The Wiz* (1978), an all-black version of *The Wizard of Oz* (1939) in which Dorothy (Diana Ross) must discover the value of home by negotiating the dangers of the inner city, shows the practice extending even beyond

PLATE 12 Lena Horne as Georgia Brown is the center of attention in *Cabin in the Sky* (Vincente Minnelli, 1943; Producer: Arthur Freed).

the classic studio era. In the 1930s and 1940s, independent black filmmakers made several black musical westerns, a number of them, including *The Bronze Buckaroo* (1939) and *Harlem Rides the Range* (1939), featuring baritone Herb Jeffries as a black singing cowboy. Sometimes this segregation was literally enacted: *The Pirate* featured a climactic dance sequence by Gene Kelly and black dancers The Nicholas Brothers, Fayard and Harold, dancing together to Cole Porter's song "Be a Clown," which was omitted when shown in some cities in the American South. The racism that infuses the film musical works alongside its utopian vision, for its representation of a harmonious society usually means it is populated only by white people.

Black performers were marginalized even when they appeared in films with white actors (see Gabbard, 1996). For example, black musicians did not appear in mainstream musicals as leads. In the musicals in which they appear, performers such as Louis Armstrong, Chuck Berry, and Little Richard play themselves rather than characters who are significant agents within the narrative. They exist as musical interludes within the story or as characters in subsidiary roles such as shoeshine boys (*The Band Wagon*), boiler room workers (*Shall We Dance*, 1937), or guests of the "massah" of the mansion (*High Society*, 1956) who have no significant function within the narrative's dramatic conflicts (Grant, 1986: 203).

Despite its title, astonishingly, *The King of Jazz* (1930), which purports to show the historical evolution of this music, eliminates the black contribution entirely. The film stars the fortuitously named Paul Whiteman, perhaps the most commercially successful bandleader of the 1920s. At different times he employed in his orchestra several important jazz musicians – all of them white – including Bix Beiderbecke, Frankie Trumbauer, and Red Norvo. An animated sequence at the beginning explains how Whiteman "came to be crowned the King of Jazz." The narrator tells us that the story takes place "in darkest Africa," and we see a cartoon version of Whiteman in pith helmet and bush jacket loping along, rifle in hand. As the cartoon Whiteman plays his violin, caricatured African natives strut to the beat. Whiteman is hit in the head by a coconut hurled by a mischievous monkey, which, we learn, is how he received his royal nickname. In this demeaning representation, blacks are associated with the jungle, with animals, and with primitivism, and are inspired to indulge their "natural rhythm" by the civilized white man. The film's final sequence, entitled "The Melting Pot of Music," shows how different ethnic and cultural musical influences combined to produce jazz. Scottish bagpipers, Irish tenors, and so on, perform before a giant bubbling cauldron, the "melting pot." African and Afro-American influences are noteworthy by their absence. For Krin Gabbard, *The King of Jazz* reveals "the degree to which blacks were contained in Hollywood even when they were physically present" (Gabbard, 1996: 13).

Other critics have read a range of film musicals, from *The Jazz Singer* (1927) to *Little Shop of Horrors* (1986), in terms of race. In one of the lengthiest and most nuanced analyses, Susan Smith argues that many film musicals reveal "a readiness to confront and explore ... the realities of racial and gender oppression" (Smith, 2005: 118). Smith offers several close readings of film musicals, including *Cabin in the Sky*, *A Star is Born* (1954), and *My Fair Lady* (1964), moving away from what she terms an "image-centered" analysis for a more holistic account that acknowledges musical and dance traditions, and performance and vocal style in relation to narrative and mise-en-scène. Surprisingly, even in *Showboat*, which many have condemned as racist, Smith finds in the 1951 version a problematizing of the racist complacency of the earlier 1936 adaptation (Smith, 2005: 23–4). Arthur Knight similarly argues that because of its complex network of entertainment influences, "the musical film became a locus around which crucial debates about the sound, sight, and stories of black music – and thus symbolic debates about African Americans and their culture(s) in America – could play out" (Knight, 2002: 7). Playing on the use of the term "integration" to refer to the relation between musical numbers and narrative in musicals, Knight deconstructs ("disintegrates") a number of film musicals, par-ticularly ones featuring black performers, finding in them a struggle to express black identity.

Certainly, many film musicals are ideologically conservative. They support dominant ideology in terms of race, gender, and sexuality. They promote dominant American values and myths of the American nation. They disguise their own markers of production to create an idealized sense of entertainment that, says Dyer, while "responding to needs that are real, at the same time . . . is defining and delimiting what constitute the legitimate needs of people in this society" (Dyer, 1980: 184). Nevertheless, "genres are not blindly supportive of the cultural status quo," as Schatz reminds us. He points out that the narrative resolution alone does not tell the complete story, ideologically speak-ing, and that "the nature and articulation of the dramatic conflicts leading to that climax cannot be ignored." Schatz concludes by asserting that "genres function as much to challenge and criticize the values that inform them." As Smith's analyses demonstrate, film musicals, like all genre films, have the ability "'to play it both ways,' to both criticize and reinforce the values, beliefs, and ideals of our culture within the same narrative context" (Schatz, 1981: 35).

And so it is to a consideration of how specific important film musicals continually renegotiate "the tenets of American ideology" (Schatz, 1981: 35) that we now turn.

CHAPTER 3

GOLD DIGGERS OF 1933 (1933)

In the 1930s, the Great Depression called into question the validity of American capitalism, and its mythic expression, the American Dream – that nexus of cultural values, supposedly attainable by any citizen, equating happiness, material wealth, career success, and bourgeois comfort. Attuned to the cultural *zeitgeist*, Warner Bros emphasized the production of two genres, the gangster film and the musical. Both genres were largely urban and both dealt with the question of "making it," but they depicted their respective characters' relation to society in opposite ways. The individualism and expansive optimism of American mythology was fueled by the open spaces of the American frontier, but by the 1920s, when the gangster film as a distinct genre began to take shape with Josef von Sternberg's *Underworld* (1927) and *Thunderbolt* (1929), the frontier was already consigned to history, officially declared closed following the census of 1890. The gangster film constituted, on one level, a cultural response to the closing of the frontier, for its protagonists embraced a pioneer individualism placed in a contemporary setting. These movies remained remarkably American in spirit with their celebration of a new breed of Robber Barons seeking the American Dream amid the dangers and opportunities of the urban wilderness. In both the movies and the real world, the closing of the frontier, that space which historian Frederick Jackson Turner (1961) argued was so important as a social and economic "safety-valve" for the American psyche, was followed by the opening of the bootleggers' spigots.

The Hollywood Film Musical, First Edition. Barry Keith Grant.
© 2012 Barry Keith Grant. Published 2012 by Blackwell Publishing Ltd.

If, as President Calvin Coolidge had declared, "The chief business of the American people is business," then, even during the Depression, business continued, at least in gangster movies.

The gangster is primarily a loner, always striving to rise to the top of the gang, but the thrust of musicals, as discussed in the previous chapter, is communal. And if the gangster film is a corruption of the American Dream, the musical film has the potential to express its fulfillment. Thus, in the 1930s, musicals proved to be a particularly amenable genre for at once both addressing and escaping the urgent problems of the Great Depression, into which the United States had precipitously plunged not long after the appearance of *The Jazz Singer* in 1927. Bursting forth in song implied optimism, an important message at the time, and the very nature of dance suggests a sense of social harmony, for dancing partners move in step with each other. And while dance was a useful metaphor of communal order, the lavish spectacles created by Hollywood musicals also took audiences' thoughts away from the economic deprivations in their own lives.

Gold Diggers of 1933 was put into production shortly after *42nd Street* (1933), which was the top film at the box office in the first half of the year (Hoberman, 1993: 67). It used the same backstage formula as the earlier film and reunited several of the same stars, including Ruby Keeler, Dick Powell, Ginger Rogers, Guy Kibbee, and Ned Sparks, while adding William Warren, Joan Blondell, and Aline MacMahon. Warners' generic strategy worked, for *Gold Diggers* was the second top-grossing film of 1933 (Hoberman, 1993: 67). Several of the film's stars would quickly be united yet again for *Footlight Parade* (1933) and also for the "sequels" *Gold Diggers of 1935* and *Gold Diggers of 1937*, each coming two years apart. The film's star power is emphasized immediately in the opening credits, which offer individual cameo close-ups of each of the leading actors with a coin in the background, before the overture segues into "We're in the Money" and we see another close-up of Ginger Rogers, this time singing the prelude to the song in what we will momentarily discover is, disappointingly, only a rehearsal.

The first production number in *42nd Street*, "Shuffle Off to Buffalo," acknowledges the obligatory romantic union between Peggy (Ruby Keeler) and Billy (Dick Powell), but this union is not only that of the romantic couple but also the larger union of the nation itself during the economic crisis of the Depression. This pattern informs many of the Warner Bros' musicals of the period, including *Gold Diggers of 1933*. This latter film is thoroughly steeped in the Depression ethos, with the script, by James Seymour and Erwin S. Gelsey, being written during the presidential campaign and released in the same year that Franklin Delano Roosevelt was inaugurated as the country's 32nd president. *Gold Diggers of 1933* opened in Los Angeles and New York in the same week that the National Recovery Administration (NRA), set up by Roosevelt to fight the Depression, was passed by Congress (Hoberman, 1993: 68). Just as Roosevelt was elected in the hope of renewing the optimism in America that was lost during the preceding years of Herbert Hoover's presidency, promising a "New Deal" for America, so the film, a big box-office hit, itself became an example of stimulating the economy — the perfect instantiation of Warner Bros' promotional angle when it was released: "A New Deal for Entertainment."

Gold Diggers of 1933 was directed by Mervyn LeRoy with musical numbers staged and choreographed by Busby Berkeley. The five songs featured in the film (four of which were production numbers) were written by the team of lyricist Al Dubin and composer Harry Warren, who also wrote the music for *42nd Street*. Warner Bros also used the song "We're in the Money" as the title song for a "Merrie Melodies" animated cartoon the same year. In the cartoon, toys in a department store sing and play the song after hours, when all the people are gone. The coins themselves, standing on edge in a cash register, sing "We are the money/Gotta lend us, spend us, keep us rolling along," with a Gold Eagle coin leading the choir of Abraham Lincoln on the penny, the Indian head on the nickel, and Columbia, the female personification of America, on the dime. As will be shown, the upbeat, optimistic message of *Gold Diggers of 1933* is as clear as it is in the cartoon.

Mervyn LeRoy was a studio stalwart, a contract director working mostly at Warner Bros, with a period as head of production at MGM, and directing in his career more than seventy films. He made several classic dramatic films, including *Little Caesar* (1931), *I Am a Fugitive from a Chain Gang* (1932), and *The Bad Seed* (1956), but he concentrated on lighter fare, including comedies and musicals such as *Broadway Babies* (1929), *Show Girl in Hollywood* (1930), *Million Dollar Mermaid* (1952), and *Gypsy* (1962). He also worked, uncredited, on *The Wizard of Oz* (1939). LeRoy's work has generated some critical commentary, but the prevailing attitude toward him is perhaps best summed up by Andrew Sarris, who remarks that, "As long as he is not mistaken for a serious artist, LeRoy can be delightfully entertaining" (Sarris, 1968: 184). Still, if the narrative of *Gold Diggers of 1933* seems particularly unpretentious, it is, as we shall see, thematically rich nonetheless.

The story is based on Avery Hopwood's play *The Gold Diggers*, which ran on Broadway from 1919 to 1920, and was produced by David Belasco, one of the most important figures of the New York stage.

The play was made into a silent film by Belasco in 1923, and again as a talkie, *Gold Diggers of Broadway*, which was the biggest film at the box office in 1929. As noted above, *Gold Diggers of 1933* contains only five songs, but it is considered one of the early classics of the genre. In 2003, the film was selected for preservation in the United States National Film Registry by the Library of Congress as being "culturally, historically, or aesthetically significant."

The "gold diggers" of the title are four aspiring actresses – Carol (Joan Blondell), Fay (Ginger Rogers), the *ingénue* Polly (Ruby Keeler), and the wise-cracking Trixie (Aline MacMahon) – and their materialist designs are not glossed over in the movie, which was made after the introduction of the Production Code in 1930 forbade references to extra-marital sex, but a year before its serious enforcement. So, for example, the film includes such comic lines as when Fay, thinking about making a good impression on the producer Barney Hopkins (Ned Sparks), muses, "If Barney could see me in clothes –," and is interrupted by Trixie, who interjects "He wouldn't recognize you." Then, as Carol dresses for the audition with Barney, taking Fay's dress, borrowed from a drug store for her job as hostess there, she says she is also a hostess and has "got to entertain Barney with the idea of putting us to work," implying that her intention is to prostitute herself if necessary to get them jobs. Shortly thereafter, when Barney comes into the girls' apartment, he notices Trixie, whose backside is turned to him, and comments, "I've seen that face before." As witty as they lines are, they are also relevant thematically, for as the story unfolds, the women will use their sexual appeal to manipulate the men in a number of ways.

The narrative begins with a rehearsal for a stage show, which is interrupted by a squad of men from the sheriff's office who close down the show the day before opening night because of unpaid bills. "Nowadays," Trixie says, "shows close before they open," to which Fay adds, "It's the Depression, dearie." To illustrate the point, there is a cut to a tilt shot down a sign at the theater ticket agency indicating "closed" next to the name of every theater. The general economic situation is connected to the specific characters in the next shot, in which, several months later, the girls' landlady slips a rent notice under the door of their threadbare apartment. Waking up, Polly, Carol, and Trixie joke about not having any bread. Although this isn't true, obviously times are tough, and Trixie uses fireplace tongs to steal a bottle of milk from a neighbor's fire escape through the window while Carol reminisces about better days ("a penthouse on Park Avenue with a French maid"). Fay enters, wearing dark glasses because she owes the landlady back rent, to announce that Barney is producing a new show, and the girls excitedly scurry to spruce up

Carol for the audition. In the plot, then, the new show is quickly and explicitly offered as an antidote to the doldrums of the Depression.

Carol comes back to the apartment with Barney, who has a great show and wants to hire all the women ("I'm gonna use all the girls I used before," he says self-reflexively, referring to *42nd Street*), but he lacks the money to mount it. Barney accidentally hears Brad Roberts (Dick Powell), the girls' neighbor and Polly's boyfriend, playing the piano. Invited over, Brad sings and plays "I've Gotta Sing a Torch Song," which, of course, is also meant for Polly personally. "Say, have you got something like a march?" asks Barney, and Brad picks out the beginning of the "Remember My Forgotten Man" melody. It just so happens that he got the idea the night before while watching a breadline, he explains, and Barney enthuses that the show will be all about the Depression. He likes Brad's music so much, in fact, that he exclaims, "Cancel my contract with Warren and Dubin!"

Brad offhandedly offers Barney the necessary $15,000 in cash to back the production. Of course, they all think Brad is joking in bad taste ("Say, what does he use? I'll smoke it too," cracks Trixie). But Brad insists that he is serious about backing the show as long as Polly is featured in it; he refuses to perform in it himself even though Barney thinks he has a fresh, new personality. The scene fades out as Brad goes back to his apartment, plays the "Remember My Forgotten Man" theme more insistently, and Barney rhapsodizes about the potential of the production, saying, "Gee, don't it get ya?" The next day, Brad comes through with the money, and the show, entitled "Forgotten Melody," goes into production.

The next shot shows rehearsal for "Pettin' in the Park," with Brad instructing Gordon (Clarence Nordstrum), the "juvenile," how to sing it with pep. "I've been a juvenile for eighteen years, and you're going to tell me how to sing a song?" Gordon protests, but Brad is obviously more fit "for a little exercise," as the lyrics put it. Barney agrees, and wants Brad to sing it, but Brad is steadfast about "no public appearances." The girls are suspicious that he must be a criminal to have so much money yet want to stay out of the limelight. As it turns out, Brad is in fact a millionaire's son whose family does not want him associating with lowly theater types. But on opening night, in order to save the show when Gordon is unable to perform because his lumbago has him unable to stand straight, Brad finally agrees to play the lead role. As the "Remember My Forgotten Man" march plays to a full house, Trixie explains to Brad that he has to go on because all the girls have rehearsed their hearts out for the last six weeks, and because they gave up other jobs that they can never get back. She urges him not to think only of himself, and Brad agrees, admitting that he "hadn't thought of it in that way." Polly thanks him through his dressing room door as "The Shadow Theme" plays diegetically behind them, indicating that their romance has progressed to the next level now that he has revealed himself to be a selfless trouper.

On the opening night of the show, between the musical numbers that constitute the show's great set pieces, the plot thickens. Brad is recognized, and the next day the girls, eating breakfast in remarkably improved circumstances, read the headline in the newspaper: "Boston Blue Blood Found Incognito in Broadway MUSICAL SHOW." Brad's brother, J. Lawrence Bradford (William Warren), and the family lawyer, Fanuel H. Peabody (Guy Kibbee), come to New York to prevent him from becoming involved in "this theater business" and being seduced by "gold diggers" and "parasites." Brad explains that music is his career, not banking. He wants to compose popular music, not classical music like that played by the Boston Symphony ("You've got to be half-dead to compose that"), scandalizing his brother and evoking the tension between high and low culture that informs so many musical films since *The Jazz Singer*. For Jane Feuer, Hollywood musical films frequently depict a narrative conflict between elite and popular art, which she calls "the opera vs swing" narrative. As she explains, "The particular syntax opposing popular and elite elements arises out of the genre's overall rhetoric of affirming itself by applauding popular forms" (Feuer, 1993: 54–6).

This is exactly what happens in *Gold Diggers of 1933*. Popular music – the kind of music featured in this film – warms the blood of the "back bay codfishes" and melts the class prejudice of the Boston Brahmins. First, Brad announces that he will marry Polly, even though his brother threatens to cut him off financially. Barging into the women's apartment upon his arrival in New York, the priggish and smug Lawrence mistakes Carol for Polly, and Carol is so offended by his presumptuous attempt to buy off a "cheap and vulgar" showgirl that she pretends to be Polly in order to show him up. Later, though, Lawrence melts when he dances with Carol, with whom he falls in love, and, as "We're in the Money" plays in the background, he confesses to her that he now thinks of dancing as delightful rather than vulgar. At the same time, the streetwise Trixie moves in on "Fanny" the lawyer, whom she quickly perceives as an easy target. Immediately flirting with him, she asks for a cigarette, and then attempts to give him back the cigarette and keep the gold case. But what starts as pure gold-digging turns into more genuine feelings. And so, in the end, all three couples are united. Highbrow and lowbrow, rich and poor, come together and the show goes on (Plate 13).

PLATE 13 *Gold Diggers of 1933*: The Boston lawyer Fanuel H. Peabody (Guy Kibbee) and the New York showgirl Carol (Joan Blondell) begin to get acquainted (Mervyn LeRoy, 1933; Producer: Robert Lord).

The opening number of the film, "We're in the Money," makes clear the metaphoric connection between the theatrical show and the economy, as the chorines, dressed in costumes representing coins and singing about being financially flush, are interrupted by men from the sheriff's office repossessing the costumes, sets, and equipment the day before opening night because the producer has failed to pay his bills.

The sequence may unintentionally reveal the truth, discussed in more detail below, that women in such Hollywood spectacles (and particularly Berkeley's musicals) are treated as objects of exchange, like money, and, indeed, later in the sequence a full shot of Fay in costume reveals a coin belt around her crotch like a chastity belt. But for now we might note that what begins as escapist sentiment and spectacle is revealed as a fantasy when the sheriff abruptly appears, halts the number, and closes the show for economic reasons. As Fay sings the lyrics to the song ("We never see a headline/'Bout a breadline, today/And when we see the landlord/We can look that guy right in the eye"), the camera pans right, revealing in sequence a series of women who are similarly dressed in costumes of glittering coins that resemble medieval chain mail. The metaphor is apt, for as the film tells us, we must gird our loins in order to tough out the Depression. The shot ends with a visual gag as the camera concludes its panning motion to reveal —surprisingly – Fay again at the other end of the chorus line. The circular structure of the gag offers a visual rhyme with the round coin motif, and also suggests the close-knit group that the cast and crew become as the narrative progresses.

After Fay runs through the song, which brims with an upbeat economic message ("We're in the money/The sky is sunny/Old Man Depression, you are through"), there is a cut to a medium shot as Berkeley's choreography takes over. Chorines, initially invisible behind Fay, begin fanning their arms, all holding large coins like shields (the metaphor of medieval battle again). Not coincidentally, in the upper right-hand corner of the frame, "In God" from the phrase "In God We Trust" is visible on a still larger coin prop for the set in the background, and then later in the sequence "In God We" is seen, emphasizing the communal ideology by conflating religion, the economy, and female beauty. This idea is furthered when next we see a big dollar sign, which becomes a door that opens to give forth a series of beautiful chorines onto the stage.

Related to the opening number, the climactic musical sequence of *Gold Diggers of 1933*, "Remember My Forgotten Man," is strikingly grim for a genre supposedly focused on escapist entertainment. About neglected veterans of World War I and featuring, uniquely, wounded and maimed soldiers in its choreography, Berkeley's number was inspired by a May 1932 war veterans' march on Washington, DC. It begins with Carol, dressed as a streetwalker, seeing a hobo pick up a cigarette butt. Exchanging her fresh smoke for his butt out of sympathy, she stands under a streetlamp and begins to sing. Her plea for the audience to remember her forgotten man is picked up by a black woman in an apartment window, the camera then panning to other windows, suggesting that this is the common plight of many women ("'Cause, ever since the world's began/A woman's got to have a man"), regardless of race. A policeman with a nightstick prompts the hobo to move along, but Carol shows the cop the man's lapel with his war medal pinned to it. A parade of soldiers bursts on the scene, marching through rain and lightning, wounded, bleeding, bandaged, even carried on stretchers. A wipe takes us to a breadline, where an unending line of cold men line up for soup. The Depression has reduced once brave and selfless soldiers to a shuffling lot dependent on charity. As the song's lyrics put it, "You sent him far away/ You shouted 'Hip-hooray!'/But look at him today." One man passes a smoke to the fellow behind him as the camera tracks along the desultory queue, again connoting the importance of communal cooperation to recover from the Depression. Another wipe brings us to the impressive German Expressionist set with three arches featuring soldiers marching across on stairways in silhouette as the chorus sings about remembering these noble souls (Plate 14). As the number reaches its finale, forgotten

PLATE 14 *Golddiggers of 1933*: The final "Forgotten Man" number, a rousing salute to veterans of World War I.

men fill the stairway in front and march down as the full chorus sings the refrain. In the end, then, the musical sequences have inscribed into the film a "socially conscious" treatment of the Depression rather than an escape from it. After filming of the number was completed, Jack Warner and Darryl F. Zanuck, head of production at Warner Bros, a studio decidedly Democratic in its political sympathies, were so impressed with it that they ordered it moved to the end of the film, displacing "Pettin' in the Park."

Stylistically, Berkeley's production numbers are perfectly suited to the theme of the story. Just as the characters must pull together to succeed in their mutual effort of putting on the show, so all the chorines in the production numbers have to perform in synchronization for the visual effects to work. Emphasizing the importance of geometric patterns and shapes, Berkeley's drill-team-like dance routines, like the "Forgotten Melody" show itself, requires both individual and group effort. In the film's historical context, the show that must be, and is, successfully put on becomes a metaphor for getting the country back "on its feet." Also, in putting on the show, the dancers display a physical vitality that might be said to express the dynamic energy of the American spirit, and the lavishness of the production numbers themselves are evidence of the American Dream.

Along with the backstage narrative, the musical numbers present a message of group unity. Berkeley conducted drills for the army during World War I and trained as an aerial observer – two experiences that clearly shaped his approach to dance on film, in which the chorines are deployed in symmetrical patterns and manipulate props rather than execute traditional dance steps. In his routines, all the chorines must be precisely in step for the geometrical precision of the choreography to work – that is to say, for the larger social pattern to be discernible. As Mark Roth has pointed out, there is a striking connection between this aspect of Berkeley's production numbers and the following sentiment expressed in President Roosevelt's first inaugural address, delivered in 1933, the same year as *Gold Diggers* was released:

> If I have read the temper of our people correctly, we now realize as we have never realized before out interdependence on each other; that we cannot merely take but we must give as well; that if we are to go forward, we must move as a trained and loyal army willing to sacrifice for the good of a common discipline, because without such discipline no progress is made, no leadership becomes effective. (Quoted in Roth, 1989: 48)

The relationship between Berkeley's production numbers and Roosevelt's New Deal is made explicit in the climactic number of *Footlight Parade*, wherein the chorus girls turn over placards as if a cheering section at a football game to reveal the eagle, emblem of the NRA.

In the opening "We're in the Money" number, for no particular reason except to demonstrate the star's verbal dexterity, Fay repeats the song's lyrics in "Pig Latin" ("Ear inway the oneymay"). The moment is emphasized by Berkeley's camera as he dollies in to a big close-up of her mouth as she sings. Berkeley was the first to employ close-ups of individual dancers in a musical film, but this one is closer than most and a revealing shot in terms of Berkeley's treatment of women and the phallic gaze of the camera that characterizes it. After Fay finishes her Pig Latin rendition, the camera pulls back to an extreme long shot, revealing the full chorus line for the first time as the dancers wave their large coins in undulating waves, the mise-en-scène connoting feminine softness and pliability as well as money. Despite Fay's claim in her singing that she can look "Old Man Depression" in the eye, women are positioned in the film visually as objects of the heterosexual male gaze, "legal tender," like the coins, in a patriarchal exchange system. Women may exploit this system of male privilege, as they do in the narrative, but the film's style suggests otherwise. As Fay sings, there is an abrupt cut to the sheriff and men coming into the theater to "make it snappy." They barge through the organized lines of the chorines as they dance, metaphorically penetrating and disrupting them. As Trixie walks up the stairs, one of the sheriff's men tries to pull off the bustle of her costume. "We've got to take it back," he explains, to which the wise-cracking Trixie replies, "Well, that's as far back as it goes."

The revue's first production number, "Pettin' in the Park," sung by Polly and Brad, make this underlying theme surprisingly explicit. Indeed, the production number can be read as a concise ideological statement of patriarchal power as it is found in most classic musicals. Accompanying the duet, Polly taps out the tune while Brad delivers some tame scat singing of the melody before Berkeley's visuals take over. Typical of Berkeley's choreography, the song is first sung as a straightforward duet, after which he expands on the visual possibilities as the orchestra noodles with the melody. The camera dollies in to a close-up of the image of two monkeys in a cage on a box of animal crackers, then dissolves to a shot of actual monkeys preening in a cage at the zoo as a trio of singing policemen pick up on the chorus, followed by a pan to several very different couples – old and young, rich and modest – sitting on park benches with the same idea on their minds. People, like other primates, have their sexual urges, and the fact that all these couples share a similar erotic desire offers another dimension to the narrative's communal emphasis.

Rebuffing her date's erotic advances, Polly's character leaves their taxi in a huff, clearly offended. She is directed by a female police officer (Trixie) with her nightstick to a door, above which a sign indicates "Roller Skating Service – For Little Girls Who Have to Walk Home." There were no women police officers patrolling the beat in the 1930s, so rather than suggest a forward-looking gender equality in the workforce, these images instead imply the extent to which women are subsumed within patriarchy. This idea is also suggested by the crowd of women identically dressed as Polly who pour out the door in roller skates before she can enter. Apparently a lot of women have had their virtue tested. A line of policemen with their phallic nightsticks form a barrier that sends Polly into the Roller Skating Service door, all of them laughing at her predicament as she goes in. The policemen with their nightsticks connect visually with Brad's brother Lawrence and his lawyer Fanuel, both of whom, significantly, carry canes. When the two men are out with Trixie and Carol, the same song is heard played by the diegetic orchestra in the night club they are in. Fanny does in fact put his hands on the flirtatious Trixie's knee, only to be rebuffed like Brad by Polly in the production number.

Dwarf actor Billy Barty appears as a baby in a pram. With obvious Freudian overtones, he makes his presence known to the policemen with a peashooter. The pre-genital "Baby" Barty escapes from his stroller on roller skates as the line of policemen pass over him, their legs spread apart, apparently not seeing him because their gaze is directed upwards. A visual transition impossible on a real stage takes us to a snowstorm in the petting park, where the male and female dancers are engaged in a snowball fight. The chorines dance with giant snowballs beneath the crotch of a tall snowman, an image of phallic worship as deliriously surreal as the famous sequence in which the chorines wave giant bananas in Berkeley's later *The Gang's All Here* (1943).

Berkeley cuts to one of his patented overhead shots of the chorines forming kaleidoscopic patterns with their snowballs, after which Barty emerges from beneath the spread legs of one of the chorines and rolls a snowball at the camera. This allows Berkeley another transition, to a summer's day in the park as the rolling ball comes to rest at the feet of a chorine laying supine in the grass with her beau, her legs fetchingly crossed and revealing the garter at the top of her left stocking and an ample amount of thigh above it. Baby Barty gives the camera the quickest of glances, signaling his surprise at the sight, and suggesting a collusion of shared pleasure with the film spectator. The baby is quickly growing up, as are both Lawrence and Fanny.

The camera then cranes up to reveal multiple couples similarly posed. A thunderstorm rains down on the set, and, as the women rush for shelter, Berkeley provides a low-angle shot to show their legs, now tantalizingly wet. Entering a shelter, we see a cutaway of ten cubicles, each with two chorines in it. Together they lower a shade that covers them all for privacy, but the camera nonetheless provides the voyeuristic pleasure of watching twenty girls in silhouette seeming to undress. A cutaway to a smiling Barty, now wearing a sou'wester (this is, after all, Berkeley's wet dream), mirrors the male spectator's own scopophilic pleasure, and he again looks knowingly at the camera. Then, as if to enact our shared secret wish, he begins to raise the shade, but alas, by the time he does so the women are already dressed. All the men discover that their dates are now clad in metal dresses – but the canny baby saves the day by supplying Brad with a can opener with which, like Berkeley's camera, he can pry loose the hidden pleasures women hold for men.

For Nadine Wills, femininity is largely defined through the musical film genre's convention of the crotch shot. As she argues, "[T]he crotch shot is the semantic unit *par excellence* of the show musical, while the identification of the camera/audience as male and the show as female constitutes the very foundation of the show musical's syntax" (Wills, 2001: 124). In her discussion, Wills offers a distinction between the (seemingly) accidental crotch shot and the posed crotch shot, the latter of which is typified by Berkeley's camera. She offers the camera tracking through the spread legs of the chorines in the "I'm Young and Healthy" number of *42nd Street* as an ideal example of the gendered gaze of Berkeley's camera (Wills, 2001: 127), although "Pettin' in the Park" provides equal evidence that it functioned, as J. Hoberman so succinctly puts it, as a "motorized phallus" (Hoberman, 1993: 60).

Ultimately, the gender politics of *Gold Diggers of 1933* is inseparable from its economic theme. While Berkeley's voyeuristic camera provides the pleasures of erotic arousal, so the show within the film is depicted as an important economic stimulus. Just as in *42nd Street*, director Julian Marsh acknowledges that he is doing the big show for one reason only – money – so the importance of money to entertainment is established from the outset in *Gold Diggers of 1933*, with the shutting down of rehearsals. In the 1930s, men were predominately the wage earners, the breadwinners, while women's place was defined within the domestic sphere. But in the show within the film, women work along with men. Indeed, the show depends upon them. So to counter the threat that working women ("gold diggers") may be perceived as posing to the male hegemony of the workplace, they are ultimately controlled in the film as objects of the male gaze. As Lucy Fischer sums up, Berkeley's chorines "seem to extend passivity virtually into catatonia and propose the image of female as ambulatory Surrealist mannequin" (Fischer, 1980: 76).

This tension is paralleled by the film's resolution of the conflict between individual ability and group effort. For Leo Braudy, Berkeley's musicals "lack any sense of the individual" (Braudy, 1977: 142), but in his production numbers the viewer's attention is inevitably focused on the tension between the anonymous mass of symmetrical dancers and the individual dancer who may be slightly out of step. Indeed, in the second production number, "The Shadow Waltz" (Plate 15), there may be several dozen women wielding neon-lit violins in the dark, but the instrument that inevitably stands out is the weakly lit one which seems about to short-circuit. (In fact, an earthquake hit Burbank while this number was being filmed, causing a blackout that short-circuited some of the violins and almost knocking Berkeley from his perch atop the camera boom.)

PLATE 15 *Gold Diggers of 1933*: The chorines with their neon-lit violins in "The Shadow Waltz."

"The Shadow Waltz" begins with Brad in white tuxedo crooning to a blonde-wigged Polly, then fades in to the chorines, who sing the refrain. Berkeley dollies in for a close-up of a white lily in Polly's hand, then cuts to the chorines on a spiraling ramp with white dresses that evoke the flower, playing the neon violins. The lights go out, and all we see are the neon bows and violins being played. Suddenly the women reappear in their white dresses, and a high-angle shot shows them as a pulsating pattern. The last shot of the number is a tracking shot of the chorines, ending up at Brad and Polly, who tosses the lily into the water, causing the reflection to ripple as they kiss. Visually, the sequence, like the earlier musical numbers, resolves the tension between individual and group by being built of both long shots of the entire chorus line and close-ups of individual dancers. Similarly, in the narrative, while group effort is emphasized throughout, individual effort is also valorized because of the singular and necessary contributions of talented individuals such as Brad, keeping alive the Horatio Alger myth that anyone might become a success through a combination of "pluck and luck." In every respect, then, *Gold Diggers of 1933* endorses the American Dream at a time when its values were being sorely tested in American society.

CHAPTER 4

TOP HAT (1935)

In *Gold Diggers of 1933*, the producer of the show-within-the movie, Barney Hopkins, tells Polly that he remembers her from the chorus line of an earlier show and that one day she will come out of the chorus. His comment refers not only to the character of Polly, but also to Ruby Keeler, the actress who plays her and who in fact did become one of the first stars of the film musical. The same success also awaited Fred Astaire and Ginger Rogers, who emerged from the chorus line in *Flying Down to Rio* (1933), their first film together, where they dance "The Carioca."

During the 1930s, Astaire and Rogers made a series of nine very popular movies together at RKO, and to this day they remain the most famous of all movie dance teams. As discussed earlier in Chapter 2, the Astaire–Rogers musicals offered a series of model heterosexual romantic relationships in an upper-class fantasy world that seemed to ignore the deprivations of the Depression. The conflicts between the couple in the narrative are resolved when their differences are reconciled, generally through the mediating power of musical performance. The developing romantic relationship of their characters, the question of whether and when will they get together, is expressed in their dances together as well as in the unfolding of the slim plots. Astaire and Rogers danced so well together that, as Gerald Mast notes, they became "Fred and Ginger," mythic beings for whom "dance establishes, celebrates, and confirms their spiritual union, not as a metaphor for sex but for something better

The Hollywood Film Musical, First Edition. Barry Keith Grant.

than sex." It is not until *Carefree* (1938), he notes, that they end with a kiss, "because the physical dance with which the films end is a more powerful projection of feeling into physicality than the mere touching of lips" (Mast, 1987: 149). These beings, celebrated by Federico Fellini in *Ginger e Fred* (1986), co-exist in their films along with whatever particular characters Fred Astaire and Ginger Rogers happen to be playing.

Top Hat, the pair's second starring vehicle and their most popular picture, featured music written expressly for the film by Irving Berlin, one of the most celebrated of American songwriters. It premiered at Radio City Music Hall in New York City, where it broke attendance records and went on to gross $3 million on its initial release, earning more than any film of the year except for Frank Lloyd's *Mutiny on the Bounty* with Charles Laughton and Clark Gable, and becoming RKO's most profitable film of the 1930s (Croce, 1972: 78). With the exception of "The Piccolino," the songs featured in the film have become pop and jazz standards. Berlin and Astaire met while working on the film and became friends and collaborators; the composer provided songs for five subsequent Astaire films, more than any other songwriter, and considered Astaire to be the best vocal interpreter of his music. *Top Hat* was nominated for four Oscars (Best Picture, Art Direction, Original Song, and Dance Direction), although it did not win any. (*Mutiny on the Bounty* won Best Picture, while Harry Warren and Al Dubin's "Lullaby of Broadway" from *Gold Diggers of 1935* took Best Song over *Top Hat's* "Cheek to Cheek.")

The film was directed by Mark Sandrich, an important director of the period who has largely been forgotten today, eclipsed by the stars with whom he tended to work: Astaire and Rogers, of course, and also Bing Crosby (three films), Claudette Colbert (two films), and comedian Jack Benny (three films). Sandrich emerged as a director of comedies in the late 1920s, but, with an interest in the relatively new genre of musicals, he was assigned to direct *The Gay Divorcee*, Astaire and Rogers' first film as the romantic leads, in 1934. Sandrich went on to direct the two stars in three more of their films: *Follow the Fleet* (1936), *Shall We Dance* (1937), and *Carefree*. During World War II, Sandrich directed *Holiday Inn* (1942), with Astaire and Bing Crosby, and with music again provided by Berlin, including "White Christmas," one of the best-selling songs of all time.

Sandrich does not approach the film musical in a manner as distinctive as that of Busby Berkeley, nor is he an auteur who, like Vincente Minnelli or Brian De Palma, engages with the genre to express a personal vision. Rather, the "self-effacing" Sandrich (Mast, 1987: 150) seemed to have worked best as part of a creative ensemble. Such a collaboration clearly informs the making of *Top Hat*. In the dance sequences, Sandrich deferred to Astaire's approach, the opposite of Berkeley's, which was to preserve the space and time of the dances. Trained as an engineer, Sandrich constructed a special dolly to help the camera move along with the dancers and keep them centered in the frame (Furia and Patterson, 2010: 92). The choreography was created by Astaire with help from Hermes Pan, whom he met and collaborated with on "The Carioca" while filming *Flying Down to Rio*, and who would go on to collaborate with Astaire on the dances for all of his RKO musicals with Ginger Rogers.

The screenplay was co-written by Dwight Taylor, Allan Scott, and Sandrich. Taylor, who had written the screenplay for *The Gay Divorcee*, was the principal screenwriter for this first screenplay written specially for Astaire and Rogers. Scott, who would go on to serve on six of the Astaire–Rogers pictures, was hired by Sandrich to do the rewrites but never actually worked directly with Taylor. The impressive sets were designed by Carroll Clark, the unit art director on all the films Astaire and Rogers did at RKO except for their last, *The Story of Vernon and Irene Castle* (1939). Clark managed the group of designers assigned to the film and worked under the general supervision of Van Nest Polglase, to whom the film's art direction is credited. As in *The Gay Divorcee*, Edward Everett Horton serves as a comic foil to Astaire, with character actors Eric Blore as the valet Bates and Erick Rhodes as the fashion designer Alberto Beddini again providing additional comic relief. The wise-cracking Helen Broderick replaced Alice Brady. The plot of *Top Hat* relies, as does that of the earlier film, on the comic complications of mistaken identity, one of the basic conventions of romantic comedy, and is sufficiently similar to the earlier film for Arlene Croce "to qualify it as a remake" (Croce, 1972: 68).

Like Busby Berkeley's extravaganzas and the other musicals in the Astaire–Rogers series, *Top Hat* was designed as escapist entertainment for Depression audiences. Taylor himself said that the film was made in the spirit of "inconsequentiality" (quoted in Croce, 1972: 71). The sets, for which "the studio decided to shoot the works" (Croce, 1972: 76), are overwhelming triumphs of art deco fantasy, and in fact were the most costly part of the film's budget. "The Big White Set" of this utopian Venice filled two sound stages and featured a winding canal spanned by three bridges (one of which Astaire and Rogers dance across in "Cheek to Cheek") with the water dyed black and two levels of dance floors, balconies, and restaurants. The main piazza, where Astaire and Rogers dance the climactic "Piccolino," was coated in red bakelite (an early form of plastic). Supposedly this set represents the Lido, a famous European resort beach near

Venice (and venue of the annual Venice Film Festival), but, as Croce notes, "there was no reason why the locale had to be Venice – it could have been Cannes or Tangier or Monte Carlo" (Croce, 1972: 75). The set's contrived quality is hinted at in Berlin's humorous, possibly self-referential lyrics for "The Piccolino," which rhyme "Piccolino" with "bambino," "vino," and "scallopino," and explain that "[i]t was written by a Latin, a gondolier who sat in/His home out in Brooklyn." This glossy Hollywood world identified as "Italy" is pointedly different from the real Italy at the time the film was made. In 1935, that country was struggling with the effects of the Great Depression, and fascist leader Benito Mussolini was at the height of his power. In *Top Hat*'s Italy, though, there are no *fascisti* to be seen, and the people are comfortable ethnic caricatures who happily accommodate the whims of rich Americans.

Despite the film's unpretentious thematic ambitions, however, it is also a musical that does significant ideological work. In his brief structural analysis of *Top Hat*, Rick Altman identifies a number of binaries that inform the film, most of which involve themes of desire and class (Altman, 1987: 177). One might argue that these binaries inform all of the Astaire–Rogers RKO films, but receive different emphases in each movie. *Shall We Dance*, for instance, focuses more on class difference, largely mapped as an opposition of high and low culture. By contrast, *Top Hat* is primarily concerned with the definition of the ideal heterosexual couple that "Fred and Ginger" represent. In the course of the film, as their relationship unfolds, love is shown to conquer all even as masculine desire commits to monogamy, allowing for successful heterosexual partnering. Perhaps the strong communal dynamic that informed the film's production helped give *Top Hat* its mythic, ritualistic treatment of courtship and romance.

Both Alberto (Erick Rhodes), the fashion designer, and Horace Hardwick (Edward Everett Horton) display a comically inept heterosexual masculinity that elevates Fred and Ginger's relationship by comparison to that of an ideologically more perfect union. Seen in this context, the numerous gay references and jokes throughout the film, which seem at best embarrassingly cheap humor if not outright homophobia, in fact function to valorize further the mythic Fred and Ginger. Some of these jokes are at the expense of the strutting Beddini. "I am no man. I am Beddini!" he announces at one point, and at another, when Dale (Rogers) at first refuses to go to Italy with him, he declares petulantly, "No woman shall ever wear Beddini's dresses again." In the climax, when the misunderstandings are being sorted out and the bumbling producer Horace forgives Beddini, who is threatening to impale him on a sword, Alberto kisses his former nemesis in the European manner as his wife Madge (Helen Broderick) remarks, "Go right ahead, boys. Don't mind me." Many of these jokes also are aimed at Horace, the most obvious of which involve his staying in the bridal suite with Jerry (Astaire) rather than with his wife. These intimations of effeminacy are consistent with his depiction as being merely tolerated, if not dominated, by the worldly-wise Madge, who at one point gives Horace a black eye ("All I did was call her darling!").

In the narrative, Astaire plays an American dancer named Jerry Travers, who comes to London to star in a show produced by Horace. He meets and falls in love with Dale Tremont, and although she falls for him as well, she mistakes Jerry for Horace, who is married to her friend Madge, and so resists his advances (Plate 16). To flee from her own developing feelings for Jerry, she leaves for Italy with Beddini to visit Madge and to model his clothes among the smart set, but after Jerry's successful opening night performance, he follows Dale to Venice. He proposes marriage to her, but, confused by the situation, Dale agrees instead to marry Alberto. Eventually all the misunderstandings are cleared up, including Dale's marriage, which, as it turns out, never really happened because Horace's valet Bates (Eric Blore) had posed as the preacher officiating the ceremony. Now free to be together, Jerry and Dale dance off into future bliss to the tune of "The Piccolino."

Astaire's dancing in the film is not merely added to Jerry's character, but essential to it. Jerry is defined in large part through his dancing. As Gerald Mast writes, in Astaire's films, "[h]is talkies are feeties" (Mast, 1987: 153). On the level of plot, Jerry first meets Dale because his dancing disturbs her; he later identifies himself as her hansom cab driver by dancing above her; and toward the end of the film he dances again on the ceiling of the bridal suite to disturb Dale and Alberto's wedding night. Even in the dialogue, Horace is concerned that having been slapped by Dale means that Jerry might have "put his foot into a hornet's nest" of a scandal. At the very beginning of the film, after the RKO logo appears, we see Astaire's legs only, dancing, in front of a chorus line of male dancers with canes, as his name appears in the credits. The same happens with Rogers. The two pairs of legs then dance together as the image dissolves to reveal a top hat, in front of which the rest of the credits roll. This iconography became indelibly associated with Astaire and was used again in the opening of *The Band Wagon* (1953), where a hat and cane appear behind the film's credits as iconic signs of its star.

After the credits, the camera pulls back from the top hat to reveal that is on the head of one of a group of gentlemen in evening dress standing in

PLATE 16 *Top Hat*: Jerry Travers (Fred Astaire) and Dale Tremont (Ginger Rogers) during their initial comic misunderstanding (Mark Sandrich, 1935: Producer: Pandro S. Berman).

front of a building. As the overture on the sound track finishes, the music provides a few notes of "London Bridge" to help place the action. The men enter the building and the camera pans to the side of the door to the plaque identifying it as The Thackeray Club, established 1864. The shot dissolves to one of another sign inside the Club, the camera quickly dollying up to it for emphasis: "SILENCE must be observed in the club rooms." Another dissolve takes us inside one of the club's sitting rooms, where older men sit in easy chairs reading newspapers and smoking cigars as an at least equally aged waiter is soundlessly serving two of the members drinks. The liqueur glasses accidentally touch, emitting the tiniest of clinks and startling the two men. Altman observes that the club members are framed so that we do not see the lower parts of their bodies (Altman, 1987: 176); but, in contrast, as the waiter soundlessly withdraws, the camera tracks to Astaire's feet, the rest of him hidden from view by the newspaper he is reading. He clears his throat, disturbing everyone in the room. The same thing happens when he crinkles his newspaper as all the other men glare at him disapprovingly. Horace finally arrives, and quietly ushers a decidedly relieved Jerry out so they can discuss business.

Both men tiptoe out of the room, but once at the doorway to the lobby, Jerry unloads a short but furious salvo of tap steps, throwing the entire room into an uproar. Here, in this stuffy, exclusively male bastion named after the mid-nineteenth-century British novelist who affectionately satirized the foibles of the upper class in novels such as *Vanity Fair* (1847), Jerry is a brash and bumptious young American among enervated, elderly Englishmen. Yet *Top Hat* is hardly a critique of the idle rich since, as the plot unfolds, the characters are clearly having so much fun in their five-star hotels and biplanes. At most, the film offers a mild upbraiding of class privilege in the comic exchanges between Horace and his manservant Bates.

When the two men are safely back in their hotel suite, the subject quickly turns to matrimony, Horace advising Jerry that he should get married. Jerry, however, claims to prefer bachelorhood and, as he does so, the film's first song, "No Strings (I'm Fancy Free)," emerges naturally from his dialogue as Astaire makes a transition from talking to singing as smooth as his dancing. Jerry proclaims himself to be a ladies' man and boasts in response to Horace's suggestion that he has "no strings," that he's "fancy free and free for anything fancy." In song he characterizes himself as being able to make or break dates as he chooses. Then, as if to illustrate the point, as he boasts in the song, "My decks are cleared for action," Jerry begins to dance energetically, complete with spins, emphatic tap steps that recall his barrage upon leaving the Thackeray Club, and slaps on the furniture as he whirls past.

Jerry's youthful energy, expressed in opposition to the dominant ideology of heterosexual monogamy, is thus connected to the vigor of his libido through Astaire's dancing. This connection is made clear as the camera cranes down the invisible fourth wall to the room below, where Dale is in bed, linking his dancing to the intimate privacy of her boudoir in the same shot. Clearly disturbed by the noise of Jerry's dancing feet, Dale rises "from her satin pillows like an angry naiad from the foam" (Croce, 1972: 59) to complain to the hotel manager. Jerry incorporates the manager's call into his dance by escorting Horace across the room to the phone when it rings. Jerry dances so vigorously that a tile falls off the ceiling below, just missing the annoyed Dale, who marches upstairs and bursts in on an embarrassed Jerry just when he has caught a small statue of a woman that he has knocked off its pedestal. Immediately smitten, Jerry apologizes, explaining that he suffers from an "affliction" so that "every once in a while I suddenly find myself dancing." The only thing that will stop his fit, he explains, is for someone to put their arms around him, and he asks her not to leave because he feels "an attack coming on" as he breaks out into a few steps.

Finding him rude (but appealing nonetheless), Dale leaves, the melody of "No Strings" returning on the sound track, but now considerably muted. Jerry appoints himself her official "sandman," sprinkles some sand from a standing ashtray on the floor and does a gentle soft-shoe, which soothes her to sleep in the room beneath. Already Jerry's initially aggressive and indiscriminate desire is being softened by and molded to her femininity. For Croce, this is "the movie's sexiest scene." (Croce, 1972: 59) It ends on a visual gag, with Jerry's dance being so gentle that he lulls Horace to sleep and then himself too, as he slides gracefully into a chair and nods off.

The next morning finds Jerry sending dozens of bouquets of flowers to Dale's room, signing the cards "your *silent* partner." Discovering that she is leaving the hotel to go horseback riding, he takes the place of her hansom cab driver. En route, she asks the driver to go faster, and some comic banter follows as the camera pulls back from a close-up of Dale in the carriage to reveal Jerry driving. He begins to tap to the rhythm of the horse's trot – another symptom of his "affliction" – and Dale realizes his identity. Jerry confesses that he does not know how to drive the horse, but optimistically offers the adage: "In dealing with a girl or a horse, one just lets nature take its course." And, indeed, just as the horse finds its way to the stables, so too will Jerry and Dale, "Fred and Ginger," eventually come together.

And so, in the next scene, Dale's riding is interrupted by a thunderstorm that provides the pretext to bring them together. As she seeks shelter from the storm in a gazebo, Jerry pulls up in the carriage and offers her a ride, which she refuses. He climbs down and enters the gazebo, where they play out their courtship through the beautifully choreographed dance of "Isn't

This a Lovely Day (To Be Caught in the Rain)?" The choreography is one of the most eloquent instances of a challenge dance, a duet in which one does a step, the other copies it, perhaps tries to improve upon it, and so on in a kind of friendly rivalry. Here Fred and Ginger mime the to and fro of flirtation and seduction as Jerry and Dale test each other out with dance steps and then finally dance together. The sequence, like many of Astaire and Rogers' dance numbers, is shown in one continuous take, preserving space and time, the camera framing them "as perpetually symmetrical figures in a perfectly balanced frame" (Mast, 1987: 151). This visual balance expresses the harmony of their developing relationship, which, despite the comic misunderstandings that will inevitably ensue and delay it, will eventually triumph.

As the sequence begins, Jerry enters the gazebo and, with the slightest of graceful steps, skips around some puddles in the walkway, the subtle lift in his step indicating his barely contained pleasure at the opportunity to talk to Dale. She is initially aloof, but a sudden thunderclap sends her momentarily running into Jerry's arms. Jerry then explains to her what thunder is, and his description ("when a clumsy cloud from here meets a fluffy little cloud from there . . . he billows towards her") obviously relates to the ritual dance of flirtation going on between them. He slides closer to her on the word "billow" and once again smoothly segues into the introduction of the song ("The weather is frightening/the thunder and lightning . . .") which is somewhere between speech and song. As he sings that the day is wonderful despite the inclement weather because the rain has forced them together, Dale is turned away from him, but she periodically glances askance at him and secretly smiles as she begins to move her riding crop to the song's rhythm. Rogers' evolving facial expression while Astaire sings perfectly encapsulates the entire move-ment of the dance to follow, from initial resistance to capitulation to acceptance of pleasure.

After singing the song's verses, Jerry begins to dance leisurely while whistling the melody. As if against her will – but not really so – Dale picks up on the melody, suddenly stands up, and inexplicably performs the same steps as Jerry at exactly the same time. They are in sync, there seems to be a connection between them, which the rest of the dance will explore. Against the railings of the gazebo are many empty chairs and music stands awaiting a band to occupy them, but musicians are unnecessary for Jerry and Dale, who clearly hear the same non-diegetic music. John Mueller describes the choreography as expressing their initial flirtation, moving from mocking to cooperation (Mueller, 1986: 76-87). Periodically they stop in their tracks, posed momentarily, as if daring the other to do the same thing. For Croce, "Those spurting little phrases that end in a mutual freeze" seem to say "Try and catch me" (Croce, 1972; 62); but at the same time, these moments show how perfectly in step the two are, moving to the same rhythms even when on the offbeat. Recognizing the connection between them, toward the end of the dance they touch for the first time when Dale crooks her arm and Jerry immediately and instinctively knows to take it. They do some turns arm in arm, and they conclude their *pas de deux* as first he lifts and spins her, and then she does the same for him as they come to rest together on the gazebo steps. Their romantic connection is one of equals, each having discovered a kindred spirit in the other, as expressed in the handshake they exchange as the scene fades.

At this point, though, Jerry's fancy is still too free for a suitable match with Dale. When Horace suggests to Jerry that Dale had slapped him in the hotel lobby because of some lack of decorum in the heat of the moment, Jerry promptly replies, "Well, if I did, I'm going right down and do it again." However, Dale has already checked out, as Jerry discovers upon going to her room, and the scene ends on a close-up of his many flowers being stuffed into the wastebasket by the maid, an apt image of his dashed hopes. The story shifts to Jerry's show that evening, which begins with the image of the flowers being tapped into the wastebasket dissolving to a close-up of the conductor in the theater pit tapping his baton as he leads the orchestra into the song "Top Hat, White Tie and Tails." Then, backstage, we find out that this is the beginning of the second act of Jerry's new show, already a hit. A telegram from Madge reveals that, coincidentally, Dale is visiting her in Italy, and Jerry insists that if Horace wants the show to continue its anticipated long run, he will have to charter an airplane to take Jerry to Italy for the weekend. When a flustered Horace asks what kind of plane, Jerry responds, "One with wings," as he glides out his dressing room door toward the stage.

The number begins with a male chorus dressed in formal wear strutting in step, with a stylized backdrop featuring the Eiffel Tower in the background (Plate 17). The Parisian setting is as arbitrary as the Venetian location to follow, although it does add a sense of romantic sophistication to Jerry, who now appears singing that he is "dusting off his tails" because he has received "an invitation through the mails." He holds the telegram from Madge in his hand, so the production number, although ostensibly part of his show, is clearly about his developing relationship with Dale. He sings Berlin's famous line, "I'm stepping out, my dear, to breathe an atmosphere that simply reeks with class," recalling Jerry's previous unfortunate encounter with "class" in the Thackeray Club. Sure enough,

PLATE 17 *Top Hat:* Fred Astaire and the male chorus dance to Irving Berlin's "Top Hat, White Tie and Tails."

he promises that once there he will be "stepping on the gas," mussing his white tie because he will be dancing in his tuxedo.

As if to emphasize the point, Jerry unleashes a few energetic tap steps, echoed by the chorus, to begin the dance. Soon the chorus leaves the stage to Astaire, who dances solo for the first time on film with his cane as a prop.

By slapping his cane on the dance floor to complement the syncopated rhythms of his tap shoes, Astaire suggests that Jerry continues to willfully flout decorum. The chorus then returns, and Jerry proceeds to "kill" all of them, using the cane as a rifle and a machine gun, his feet tapping out the sounds of the shots, and lastly as a bow and arrow. The odd choreography at this point suggests Jerry's potency and a primal sense of male competition, but with a veneer of civilized manners ("putting in the shirt studs/polishing my nails").

The number ends as it began, with a shot of the conductor leading the orchestra, now reprising Berlin's tune. The shot in turn dissolves to a band in Venice playing the same song as the camera then tracks along the canal of the sumptuous set to find Dale, with Bates surreptitiously following her as ordered earlier by Horace. In her comic misunderstanding with Madge about Jerry's identity, Dale confesses that "Horace" chased her in the park. Curious, Madge asks, "Did he catch you?" and Dale's reluctantly affirmative response really means that, yes, she has fallen in love with him. Now it is Dale's turn to be counseled by her elder, and Madge tells her that despite the fact that all men are male, it is important to marry one who is reliable. Shortly thereafter, Jerry tells Horace that he is going to marry Dale.

In a nightclub that evening, the camera cranes in to Madge and Dale's table as couples dance about them to the strains of "Cheek to Cheek." Jerry joins them, the comic misunderstanding persisting as Madge encourages them to dance together, telling Dale to pay her no mind. They begin to dance, Jerry putting his arm around Dale's waist and leading her onto the floor just as the music plays what we will soon know as the accompaniment to the lyric "Dance with me/I want my arm about you." While they dance, Jerry begins to sing his dialogue, as with "No Strings." Presumably, the source of the music is an unseen orchestra playing in the nightclub, yet it seems to be accompanying Jerry's singing, and none of the other couples dancing acknowledges his doing so. This ambiguity regarding the music's diegetic status again emphasizes the connection between Jerry and Dale – another indication, as in the gazebo earlier, that being in love means sharing private music.

During the second verse, Jerry subtly leads Dale away from the crowded dance floor and then, during the dramatic break, swings her away from and then back towards him (Plate 18), after which they dance alone on an adjacent floor. At the end of the song, they dance cheek to cheek across a bridge. It is as if they are off the ground, floating on air, as they enter a conveniently empty ballroom, spinning together. Dale's feathery dress – later parodied by Astaire in one of the numbers with Judy Garland in *Easter*

PLATE 18 *Top Hat:* Astaire and Rogers dance "Cheek to Cheek."

Parade (1948) – adds to this feeling of floating, of being "as light as a feather." This, the song suggests, is what it is to be "in heaven."

No longer merely flirting, Dale and Jerry are now in love. But Dale feels deceived by a man she thinks is already married. According to Mueller, Jerry therefore must conquer her hesitations, even without understanding them, and the choreography reflects this in its carefully designed use of the supported backbend (Mueller, 1986: 76–87), a movement which does not appear in "No Strings," the pair's previous dance together. The dance begins by briefly reprising the sequential imitation of the challenge dance; but Jerry and Dale's feelings have progressed since then, and the dance moves on to other steps. The first backbend occurs when Astaire spins Rogers and brings her back, cradling her in his arms ("I want my arm about you") and gently leaning her backward. The music picks up in tempo, and the backbend is repeated twice, each time deeper than the one before. As the music and dance come to a climax, Astaire lifts Rogers three times and concludes with the deepest backbend, which they hold momentarily before rising and briefly dancing – of course – cheek to cheek before finishing. These supple backbends emphasize Dale's surrender to her love despite her believing that he is married to her friend, thus making the dance nothing less than "a hymn to pleasure" in the face of social constraint (Altman, 1987: 173).

Subsequently, when Beddini finds Dale alone on a balcony, he proposes to her and in her confusion and loneliness she accepts, and the two swiftly undergo a marriage ceremony (which, as we will see, turns out to be a sham). But her heart wishes for "Horace," as indicated by the reprise of "Isn't It a Lovely Day," their private music, on the sound track throughout the scene. Then, when Dale learns Jerry's true identity, they dine together even though they believe this is her wedding night, while her "husband" Alberto, along with Horace and Madge, are out in a motorboat futilely searching for them in the fog, with Bates having "taken the precaution of removing the gasoline." Jerry further flaunts conventional morality when he declares, "Let's eat, drink, and be merry, for tomorrow we have to face him." For Altman, the viewer is seduced by the socially unsanctioned pleasure the loving couple embrace, but it is important to remember that the narrative contrives to allow it only by repositioning Jerry's "free fancy" to the "strings" of heterosexual monogamy. As the experienced Madge advises Dale, "No husband is too scared too look" – but the important thing is not to "clear the decks for action."

Upon Jerry's exhortation to "eat, drink, and be merry," the music of "The Piccolino," the film's big finale, begins. A convoy of gondolas is followed by a chorus consisting of many identically dressed couples who do ballroom steps choreographed by Hermes Pan. Berlin conceived of the number in the climactic spirit of "The Carioca" from *Flying Down to Rio* and "The Continental" in *The Gay Divorcee*. The shot of the chorus of dancing partners changes with a rare wipe to a high-angle shot of them moving in geometrical patterns in a parody of Busby Berkeley. There is a cut to Jerry and Dale, as she begins singing the song to him. Once again there is an ambiguity as to the music's diegetic status. Dale's song is followed by a montage of Berkeley-like shots of the dancing chorus connected by a series of wipes. It begins with a shot of the dancers in the background obscured by a female dancer's shapely legs in the foreground – a joke about the more suggestive aspects of Berkeley's choreography, as discussed in the previous chapter.

Then a shot of Astaire and Rogers dancing the Piccolino begins with a close-up of their legs as they get up from their dinner table. The shot unfolds into a long take of two minutes showing the entire dance, the chorus now in still poses behind them. Stylistically, their dance is presented in marked contrast to the chorus's dance: where the shots of the chorus are long shots of short duration with the camera stationary in each, the shot of Jerry and Dale dancing is a full shot of long duration with the camera gracefully gliding to keep them centered in the frame as they move across the floor. The Piccolino step, which involves the feet darting out to the side of the body, recalls Jerry's joyful skipping past the puddles before his first dance with Dale in the gazebo. As the dance finishes, the couple move smoothly back to their table with several flourishes of the Piccolino kick and conclude by lifting their glasses in a mutual toast that seals their union. Then, once everyone comes together and the misunderstandings are clarified, including Dale and Alberto's fake marriage, the last obstacle to Jerry and Dale's union is overcome. In the brief reprise of "The Piccolino" that ends the film, the couple dance across one of the bridges of the Venetian set, reprising the kick step, and off into a blissful future, spinning out of the frame to live happily ever after as this final shot fades out on the screen and into the spectator's imagination.

CHAPTER 5

THE PIRATE (1948)

The Pirate, directed by Vincente Minnelli, is one of the important film musicals produced by Arthur Freed for MGM. As discussed in Chapter 1, the Freed Unit was responsible for many of the studio's best musicals, including *Meet Me in St Louis* (1944), *Singin' in the Rain* (1952), and *The Band Wagon* (1953), all of which consciously aimed to integrate the musical numbers at the level of narrative and theme. Minnelli himself said that in musical films the "numbers should be given as much importance as dramatic sequences" (Higham and Greenberg, 1972: 199). *The Pirate* is one such integrated musical, as it fuses its visual, narrative, and musical elements into a coherent, if stylistically delirious, whole. The film provides its own aesthetic self-justification, its patent and excessive stylization a function of its protagonists' romantic vision. As Dana Polan puts it, the film reveals a "mastery of spectacle in which gliding cameras, radiant Technicolor, the texture of songs, all have the force of an argument for a style and way of life, for life as style and as art" (Polan, 2009: 136).

The Pirate stars Gene Kelly and Judy Garland, and was their first film together since *For Me and My Gal* (1942), Kelly's debut, several years earlier. The screenplay was written by the married team of Frances Goodrich and Albert Hackett based on S.N. Behrman's non-musical comedy, produced on Broadway in 1942 and itself adapted from an earlier comedy of the same name written by German playwright Ludwig Fulda. Goodrich and Hackett also wrote the screenplays for *Easter Parade* (1948),

The Hollywood Film Musical, First Edition. Barry Keith Grant.
© 2012 Barry Keith Grant. Published 2012 by Blackwell Publishing Ltd.

again starring Judy Garland, and *Seven Brides for Seven Brothers* (1955), two other Freed Unit musicals, as well for several important dramatic films, including Frank Capra's cult classic *It's a Wonderful Life* (1946). The choreography was created by Kelly and Robert Alton, a dance director at MGM in the late 1940s and a Broadway choreographer who is credited with discovering Kelly and making him a star in the original stage production of *Pal Joey* in 1940. The music for *The Pirate*, featuring five songs by Cole Porter, was nominated for an Academy Award for Original Music Score, but lost to *Easter Parade*.

Minnelli, who was married to Garland at the time they made the film, is known primarily for a number of musicals in addition to *The Pirate*, including *Cabin in the Sky* (1943), *Meet Me in St Louis*, *An American in Paris* (1951), *The Band Wagon*, and *Brigadoon* (1954). But he was also the director of several notable melodramas, including *Madame Bovary* (1949), *The Bad and the Beautiful* (1953), *The Cobweb* (1955), and *Some Came Running* (1958). Minnelli's attraction to these two genres is hardly coincidental. Most obviously, the very term "melodrama," literally meaning a combination of music (*melos*) and drama, points to that genre's association with excessive ("operatic") stylistics, which also informs many film musicals. But in the case of Minnelli, the connection between the two genres works at a deeper level. As Thomas Elsaesser noted back in 1970, Minnelli's melodramas "are musicals turned inside out, for the latter affirm all those values and urges which the former visualize as being in conflict with a radically different order of reality" (Elsaesser, 1981: 17). In the case of *The Pirate*, Robin Wood has pointed out the connections between Manuela Alva (Garland), the film's female protagonist, and Emma Bovary, the heroine of Gustave Flaubert's famous novel, which, as we have seen, Minnelli was to adapt as a melodrama for his next film the following year. Wood argues that both women are trapped within bourgeois, patriarchal society and respond by entertaining romantic fantasies of escape (R. Wood, 2009: 155–7).

Because of his opulent visual style – so clearly in evidence in *The Pirate* – Minnelli is often dismissed as a stylist, someone more interested in décor than depth, a *metteur-en-scène* rather than an auteur. Thus Andrew Sarris, even while acknowledging that Minnelli "had an unusual, somber outlook for musical comedy," nevertheless concludes that the director "believes more in beauty than in art": "If he has a fatal flaw as an artist, it is his naïve belief that style can invariably transcend substance and that our way of looking at the world is more important than the world itself" (Sarris, 1968: 101–2). However, as the following discussion of *The Pirate* will show, Minnelli's style is inextricable from his "somber outlook," for the film's fantastic style functions as a visualization of its heroine's repressed desire, itself a reaction to the bourgeois and patriarchal society in which she lives.

The plot of *The Pirate* centers on a young woman, Manuela, who lives in the small Caribbean village of Calvados, in the 1830s, and who dreams of being swept away by the legendary Pirate, Mack "the Black" Macoco. However, her Aunt Inez (Gladys Cooper) and Uncle Capucho (Lester Allen), who have raised her, have arranged her marriage to the town's mayor, Don Pedro Vargas (Walter Slezak), a corpulent blowhard. Manuela convinces her aunt to take her to the nearby town of Port Sebastian, where her wedding dress will be arriving by ship. At the same time as they come to the bustling port town, a troupe of traveling actors and acrobats also arrives. Their spirited leader, Serafin (Kelly), promptly heads off to flirt with all the girls – until he encounters Manuela, with whom he immediately falls in love. Serafin attempts to charm Manuela out of marrying Don Pedro, but while Manuela clearly enjoys the attention from him, she hurries away out of propriety.

That night, however, Manuela is unable to sleep, and hearing the clamor of the players on the street, she sneaks out to see Serafin's show. During the performance, Serafin sees Manuela and hypnotizes her so that she will admit her love for him. But instead, in a trance, she madly sings and dances about her love for the notorious pirate. When Manuela awakens and realizes what has happened, she is aghast and once again flees the scene.

On Manuela's wedding day, the traveling troupe arrives in Calvados. Serafin finds Manuela, climbs in through her balcony window, and pleads with her to admit that she really loves him and to join the troupe. Don Pedro arrives and, enraged, orders Manuela to leave as he prepares to whip the actor. But Serafin recognizes Don Pedro as Macoco, now grown fat and desperately trying to lead the life of a respectable citizen. He blackmails Don Pedro, threatening to reveal the mayor's true identity if he does not relax his ordinance against outsiders and allow his troupe to put on their show. In order to win Manuela, Serafin also pretends to be the famous brigand, causing the entire town to cower in fear. When he threatens to burn down the town, Manuela agrees to go with him; comically, she pretends to be a martyr who has accepted her fate for the greater good, walking slowly, head bowed, as if to her death, but secretly happy. At the last minute, she accidentally discovers the truth about Serafin, and, in revenge, she first pretends to seduce him, as if under the spell of his macho posturing, and then attacks him physically. When she accidentally knocks him out, though, she realizes that she really does love him.

Meanwhile, Don Pedro goes to the capital and returns with the Viceroy (George Zucco) and his militia to arrest the wanted "Macoco."

He convinces the Viceroy that Serafin is the real Macoco by planting some of his booty in the actor's prop trunk. Serafin is arrested and is sentenced to hang. At the execution, Manuela looks at the evidence and notices a bracelet with the same design as the engagement ring Don Pedro had given her, thus realizing that he is the real Macoco. As his last request, Serafin asks to do one final show before his sentence is carried out, with the plan of hypnotizing Don Pedro into revealing his true identity. But Aunt Inez intervenes and breaks the mirror. Then, thinking quickly, Manuela pretends to be hypnotized and proclaims her complete devotion to Macoco, causing Don Pedro to boil over with jealousy, leap onto the stage, and declare that he is in fact the infamous pirate. He seizes Manuela while brandishing a pair of pistols, but Serafin's troupe attacks Don Pedro with juggling pins and other stage props, disarming him. In a coda, Manuela, now part of the troupe, joins Serafin on a stage for a reprise of "Be a Clown," which was performed shortly before with the astonishingly acrobatic Nicholas Brothers, Fayard and Harold, as part of Serafin's "final performance."

As this plot summary suggests, *The Pirate*, like so many musicals, is built around the formation of a romantic union between a heterosexual couple, but it is arguably the story only of its female protagonist. That is to say, *The Pirate* is a subjective narration by Manuela in which Serafin is not a "real" character at all but represents her sexual fantasies. The very first image in the film after the credits is a point-of-view shot from Manuela's perspective showing her hands holding a book about pirates as we hear her voice reading the text aloud to her friends, rhapsodizing about Macoco, "whose glorious and formidable exploits are here related in a true history staggering to the imagination and ravishing the sensibilities." On the cover of the book is the title, "The Pirate," the same title as the film itself, ornately embossed in gold. The extravagantly stylized font, with its swooping swirls stemming from the letters "R" and "A" in the word "Pirate," points to the heavy stylization of the film it is also announcing.

As Manuela reads, her hands turn the book's pages and we see several illustrations. Doris Lee's paintings are reminiscent of painter Paul Gaugin's in their "primitive" boldness and coloration. Not only is this the first of several instances in the film where painters are invoked, but here in the opening scene the reference is particularly important because Gaugin's South Pacific paintings carry strong associations of the romantic and adventurous escape from (European) civilization that defines Manuela's imagination. One illustration shows Macoco's ship in battle on the high seas, while the next shows him ravaging five women, with still another tied to the mast in her bloomers. Manuela's perspective in the film to follow is clearly colored by these romantic images of Macoco (later in the film when, believing Serafin to be the famous pirate, she swoons to the floor when he lightly kisses her hand), and Serafin is visualized in *The Pirate*'s subjective perspective as being like him.

As Manuela puts the book down, she continues speaking in the same purple prose as the book: "On the moving waters of the Caribbean he darts about, like a dragonfly, glittering, uncapturable." The other girls laugh at her hyperbole, more pragmatically dismissing Macoco as a common thief and declaring their preference for sensible young men who will provide them with a plantation and financial security. Then, just as Manuela chides her friends for lacking what she calls "spirituality," Aunt Inez enters to announce plans for her niece's wedding. This opening scene is visually unremarkable compared to what follows, but in the next scene, when Manuela and her aunt arrive in Port Sebastian, the style of the pirate book blossoms into the style of the film itself.

Visually, Port Sebastian is full of activity and people, a dizzy mélange of influences – "an international port which took its colors from many different countries," as Minnelli described it (Higham and Greenberg, 1972: 203), When Serafin masquerades as Macoco, he tells Don Pedro, "You should try underplaying some time. Very effective" – but this advice in fact applies to nothing else in the film, least of all the bravado of Serafin himself as Kelly so broadly plays him. Not coincidentally, the caravan of the players, as if called from Manuela's subconscious, arrives with a rousing fanfare. Manuela's song after she is hypnotized becomes an expression of her subconscious desires, repressed out of her family duty to marry Don Pedro. She wishes for a dashing and dominating romantic figure to sweep her off her feet and carry her away, but also to treat her chivalrously, "like a queen." The remainder of the film works to present Serafin exactly in this way.

Tellingly, Serafin disembarks from the same ship as the one containing her trousseau, in fact on top of the box containing it as it is being unloaded. He is lowered to the ground with the box in the rigging like a *deus ex machina* coming to "swoop" Manuela away, as she has imagined Macoco would do. "We bring to this new world all the joy, the dexterity, the romance of the old, to please, astonish, and delight you," Serafin declaims, not unlike the book's description of the pirate's tale moments earlier. Serafin's entourage includes bagpipe-playing dwarfs, jugglers, and other assorted acrobats. As Joel Siegel has noted, "Minnelli's tactic here is to supply more than the eye can absorb, to drown us in intoxicating excess" (Siegel, 1971: 27).

Although Port Sebastian is only thirty miles away from Calvados, Manuela has never seen the ocean. Upon arriving there, she immediately runs to a stone stairway on a cliff overlooking the sea to gaze out at its promise of adventures she will never have once she is married to Don Pedro. From Manuela's point of view we see two shots of the ocean, the site of her fantasies. These are the only two location shots in the entire film other than the shot of Serafin announcing his troupe's arrival from the rigging, and their relative realism underscores the intensity of Manuela's dreamworld. A tight close-up shows her rapturous face as she gazes seaward, followed by a reverse dolly to a medium shot that suddenly reveals Serafin in the frame, as if appearing out of nowhere, bidden by her secret desire. The stairway on which they meet seems higher than the sky, and apparently ends in midair, as though they are in the clouds. The clouds themselves are billowy white and unmoving in a vibrant blue sky. Serafin, having seen Manuela walking toward the sea, is immediately smitten and professes his love for her. Somehow he correctly diagnoses her inner fantasies as if he already knows her intimately.

Like the heroines of so many melodramas, including some directed by Minnelli, Manuela lives in a world constrained by money and manners. When she impulsively runs to gaze at the sea in Port Sebastian, Aunt Inez chides her by asking, "What will people think?" The film, however, shows us what Manuela thinks. For Robin Wood, money, which represents power and the potential for self-determination, is a driving force of melodrama (R. Wood, 2009: 157). In *The Pirate*, Inez's motive for arranging the marriage is purely materialistic, seemingly having little to do with love. She bargains with Don Pedro for Manuela's hand, requiring that her husband's gambling debts be paid off and that they receive an annual annuity. When Serafin pleads with Manuela on the stairway to run off with him, he asks, "Aren't you interested in love?" to which she replies, "No, I told you, I was going to be married." When Don Pedro meets with Manuela, he attempts to dismiss rather than encourage her wish for travel by telling her that they will never have to leave their village, never have to worry about the burdens of travel because he abhors the sea. "Home is the perfect spot," he declares, "so quiet, so peaceful, so safe" – an ironic comment given not only Manuela's consuming desire but also actress Judy Garland's indelible association with the character of Dorothy, who tries for most of *The Wizard of Oz* (1939) to return home for precisely these reasons. A map of the Caribbean hangs on Manuela's bedroom wall, invoking what is for her a promising place somewhere over the rainbow.

The Wizard of Oz is also invoked when Manuela flees back to her room after being hypnotized and pleads with Aunt Inez that she wants to go home, and later when Inez tells Manuela that you can make anything come true if you wish for it. These references to *The Wizard of Oz*, the first film for which Arthur Freed received credit as associate producer, are no coincidence, for like it, *The Pirate* uses a vibrant Technicolor palette to express the appeal of its protagonist's escapist fantasy and at the same time how humdrum the dreamer regards the real world in which she lives. At one point we see Manuela's image being traced for a silhouette, and, significantly, it is a dull black and white in comparison to the colorful adventure that Manuela is having with Serafin. Further, the set design of the Calvados town square and the costumes of the townsfolk in it suggest an imaginary world peopled by full-sized munchkins, an association perhaps encouraged by art directors Cedric Gibbons and Jack Martin Smith, who worked on both movies.

In the way it handles its sexual theme, *The Pirate* follows the model established by the Astaire–Rogers films. In the latter, as we have seen in the previous chapter, when the couple dance together, it is an expression that their romantic union is achieved, that masculine desire has been safely channeled into a monogamous heterosexual relationship. It is no different in *The Pirate*. Significantly, in the film, Manuela is changed from a woman already married in the play to a younger engaged woman in order to satisfy the Breen Office, enforcers of Hollywood's Production Code. As Minnelli explained, "[S]he couldn't be married to Don Pedro, obviously, for her elopement with Serafin would be considered inadmissible by the censors" (Minnelli, 1974: 184). When Don Pedro first meets Manuela before their marriage, he notes that he has watched her grow up, a line indicating the character's new, more youthful quality. Thus the film, as opposed to Behrman's play, becomes about an innocent, virginal adolescent (when she is being hypnotized, Serafin explains that it can only work with someone who is "pure") rather than an experienced woman. Despite the helpful associations of Judy Garland with adolescence, because of *The Wizard of Oz*, *Babes on Broadway* (1941), and *Meet Me in St Louis*, the fact that the film has the 26-year-old and married Garland (already the mother of baby Liza) playing a character obviously younger and so naïve merely adds to its surreal quality.

Like Astaire's Jerry Travers in *Top Hat* (1935), Serafin is initially depicted as sexually active, if not profligate, only by the end to be committed to a monogamous heterosexual relationship. While his troupe set up for the evening's performance when they arrive in Port Sebastian, Serafin promptly goes out on the town, to "survey the terrain in advance of conquest," as he says, like a sexual buccaneer, seducing and pillaging his way through the Caribbean – just like Manuela's fantasy. In the film's first song, "Niña," he expresses his desire for all beautiful women, whom he refers to with the Spanish word for the generic "girl." Before launching into the song, he explains to a curious bystander that because there are so many beautiful women in the world with so many different names, to avoid confusion he calls them all the same name which, apparently, he has chosen at random. Serafin begins the number singing, "When I arrive in any town/I look the ladies up and down," after which he will chose one and give her his "patter/no matter her name."

Gene Kelly, known as a more "virile" dancer than Astaire, sings the song while dancing with bold, athletic gestures as he climbs up and around an array of balconies, balustrades, trellises, and poles, wooing a series of women each in turn as he goes. Minnelli has said, "I never thought of anyone but Gene Kelly for the part of Serafin. Fred Astaire, even if he weren't currently retired, was too introspective to play the flamboyant swashbuckler, a pastiche – as Gene and I envisioned – of Douglas Fairbanks gymnastics and John Barrymore canned ham" (Minnelli, 1974: 184). Here, Kelly's choreography, "more an athletic feat à la Fairbanks than a dance" (Fordin, 1975: 208), exploits his gymnastic ability even more than in the film's other numbers, with the exception of the climactic "Be a Clown," performed with the Nicholas Brothers and which includes literal gymnastics such as two series of push ups as the three dancers hop on their hands and toes first right and then left. The "Niña" sequence's mise-en-scène is a riot of phallic imagery, beginning immediately with the first shot of Serafin strolling into the town square twirling a cane and smoking a cigar. At one point in the number he embraces one of the "niñas" and bends her backward through a round window frame, an image with unmistakable connotations of phallic penetration; and shortly thereafter he takes another's smoking cigarette, puts it entirely in his mouth, and kisses the woman, after which the cigarette reappears from inside his mouth, still smoking!

In his dance, Kelly accosts two proper young ladies strolling with parasols, momentarily blocking their path, combining his allure with a vague and hence exciting threat or danger – a choreographed version in miniature of the meeting that will shortly take place between Serafin and Manuela. As he flirts with the women in his dance, he gathers a chorus of female dancers who follow him, seemingly entranced, as if he were the Pied Piper, and anticipating his imminent hypnotizing of Manuela. Serafin leads the women onto a round stage with several poles serving to hold up a gazebo, as the music changes to a bolero. The arrangement now echoes Maurice Ravel's "Bolero," popularly thought of as a particularly erotic musical work (see, for example, Dudley Moore's attempt in Blake Edwards' *10* [1979] to seduce Bo Derek with a recording of it). Kelly combines classical and modern dance with pole dancing as he dances suggestively. As Joel Siegel describes the scene, "[T]he dancers whirl about the platform's poles and then, in an extraordinarily expressive movement, the camera itself begins to describe an arc around the stage" (Siegel, 1971: 27). Actually the camera moves only slightly and momentarily, but it is sufficient to suggest the erotic vertigo of a young woman in the first throes of sexual arousal. Composer Cole Porter's forced and humorous rhymes – rhyming "Niña" with "neurasthenia" and "schizophrenia," for example – are consistent with the film's parodic self-consciousness and excess in this over-the-top spectacle of a young woman's sexual awakening.

Manuela tells her Aunt, "I realize there's a practical world and a dream world. I know which is which. I shan't mix them, I promise." But try as she might to repress her fantasies for the sake of propriety, the latter inevitably merges with the former and the entire film becomes her fantasy. When she first meets Serafin on the stairway, she rebuffs him only half-heartedly, rejecting him even as she encourages him by letting him retrieve her hat, which the wind has conveniently blown off. Feigning affront, she compares him to the noble Don Pedro, whom, she insists, neither drinks nor smokes, "is regular in his church duties, and certainly wouldn't accost a young woman." But that night, she is unable to sleep and is drawn to the troupe's outdoor performance, within earshot of her room. She opens her window to see where the voices are coming from and, significantly, there is no change in the volume on the sound track, since these voices are in fact inside her rather than "out there." Later, after she finishes singing in her trance and runs back to her room, she closes the shutters of her window and this time the voices are completely muffled as she temporarily regains her composure.

At the performance, Manuela is hypnotized by Serafin, "to release her spirit from its earthly bonds," as he explains it – a fancy description of the Freudian concept of the return of the repressed. As she bursts into song, she pushes Serafin out of the way, beyond the frame of the image, as she is overwhelmed with the release of her hitherto repressed desire. Just as Serafin led a group of chorus girls in "Niña," so now Manuela gathers a chorus of male dancers around her, following her lead. She describes herself in the words Serafin had used in his description of her on the spectral stairway, saying that she has "depths of emotion" and "romantic longing" beneath her "prim exterior." The lyrics of the song recount the earlier fantasy of the pirate book as she sings that when he boards a ship, "first he grabs the ladies fair" and "ladies go to pieces over pieces of eight." Manuela's broad arm and hand gestures and her running to and fro in the choreography express the intensity of her youthful passion. The lit torches on the walls behind her during the number visually indicate that her passion has been ignited, and is a motif picked up in Serafin's pirate fantasia, discussed below. In the frenetic conclusion to "Mack the Black,"

Manuela sings that "throughout the Caribbean or vicinity/Macoco leaves a flaming trail of masculinity." She and Serafin kiss passionately before she wakes from her trance.

At the end of the number, Manuela regains consciousness and realizes with embarrassment that she has sung and danced in public. "I have nothing but horror and shame for what I did that night," she tells Serafin later, back in Calvados. She flees to her room and tries to blot out the reality of her fantasy by shutting the window and thus drowning out the boisterous applause for her performance. Robin Wood notes that window imagery is conventional in the melodrama, and that it carries an inherent ambiguity in representing both entrapment and escape (R. Wood, 2009: 164), and that is exactly how it is used in *The Pirate*. For example, on the morning of her niece's wedding, Aunt Inez flings open Manuela's shutters and announces that it's a beautiful sunny day, but the low lighting and dark shadows in Minnelli's mise-en-scène suggest otherwise; and, when Serafin is about to be wrongly executed, Inez closes the veranda windows to dampen the beating of the drums, but the shadow of the gallows' noose falls upon the shutters.

Trying on her wedding dress, Manuela opens a hat box and removes the ruined hat which Serafin had picked up for her on the stairway in Port Sebastian. She caresses it, laughing; then, catching herself, she puts the hat back in the box, and closes it. But it is too late: she has lifted the lid of her repressed desire and immediately we hear the music of the approaching players coming to Calvados. At first, given Manuela's facial expression, the sounds of their approach could be understood as a product of her imagination, non-diegetic, rather than really happening within the world of the film. This momentary ambiguity is perfectly to the point. Manuela attempts to deny Serafin by locking her door and shutting her windows, but before she can do so he sees her and walks a tightrope to the balcony of the "Fair Juliet of the Carribean" and enters her room.

Later, from her window, Manuela sees Serafin, who she now thinks is Macoco, in the town square confronting four local militia men who are about to ride to Port Sebastian for help. She shuts the window, trying to deny the sexual nature of her attraction to Serafin/Macoco, but then peaks through it. In her fevered imagination the confrontation becomes a choreographed fight as Serafin fends off all four men brandishing a cudgel. After the men flee, Serafin begins to dance around a donkey that has wandered into the square. He now wears stylized tattered pirate attire and shorts that flatter Kelly's musculature, and his cudgel has become a cutlass. A woman (Manuela?), her face hidden, has replaced the seated donkey, its ears transformed into the ends of her bandana, which at one point Serafin slices off with his cutlass as he pirouettes. The sky is a fiery red, and plumes of black smoke billow in the background. Serafin flies up to and down from the crow's nest on a tall mast amid fiery explosions and lightning flashes, then dances with a large spear. The sequence is so obviously overblown – containing all the stage effects Minnelli satirizes in Jeffrey Cordova's pompous production of *Faust* in *The Band Wagon* – and is another riot of phallic imagery. (It is worth noting that Serafin's name is unmistakably similar to "seraphim," commonly understood as "fiery serpents" in the Bible. Certainly the townspeople believe that, as the Viceroy cautions, Serafin will "strike like a cobra when he realizes he's cornered.") The music in the sequence is a frenetic version of "Mack the Black," underscoring that this is Manuela's fantasy – "precisely the sort of thing that might simmer in the libido of a properly repressed Catholic girl" (Siegel, 1971: 29).

In the extended farcical scene in which Manuela hurls the numerous furnishings in Don Pedro's parlor at Serafin, when she thinks she has knocked him unconscious after a large framed painting falls on his head (Plate 19), she stops the barrage, runs to him, and, cradling him in her arms, she calls him "darling," finally acknowledging her love for the actor. Earlier, in his masquerade as Macoco, Serafin had appropriated the phallic whip from Don Pedro; now, he rests passively, for the first time in the film, nestled in her arms as she sings to him "You Can Do No Wrong," the film's only romantic ballad. She sings that he is perfect as he is, "as right as a "nightingale's song." The reference in Porter's lyric here to John Keats' poem "Ode to a Nightingale" is particularly apt, as the poem is about listening to the beauty of the bird's song and being transported, taken away from one's worldly cares (like being "released from her earthly bonds," as Serafin describes his mesmerism). Manuela literally embraces her fantasy – a man who has the charisma of a swashbuckling pirate but who treats her like a queen, unlike the blustering Don Pedro, who presumes to order her about and who, revealing himself in the end, demands her worship. Wanting to be swooped up by a fantasy pirate, Manuela is now borne away, in Keats' words, "on the viewless wings of Poesy."

For Jean-Loup Bourget, *The Pirate* reveals a subtle social critique. As he observes,

> The actor, not the pirate, turns out to be the 'revolutionary' individual who is going to achieve social change, for he unmasks Walter Slezak..., the real Macoco who parades as a respectable citizen. The lesson is therefore that piracy can be identified with respectable bourgeois society, and that the artist (whether an actor or a Hollywood director) emerges as the one person with both a sense of individual freedom and the refusal to oppress others. (Bourget, 2003: 58)

PLATE 19 *The Pirate*: Manuela (Judy Garland) expresses her love for Serafin (Gene Kelly) by attacking him with home furnishings (Vincente Minnelli, 1948; Producer: Arthur Freed).

To be sure, it is ironic that the moral pillar of the town – "I'm very philanthropic. I repaired the church belfry," Don Pedro pleads to Serafin – is in fact the ruthless criminal responsible, according to the Viceroy, for the deaths of "thousands." And when Manuela hurls everything in her fiancé's parlor at Serafin, we might understand each smashed vase, painting, and *objet d'art* as a gesture of protest by Manuela against the comfortable bourgeois, domestic fate that awaits her if she were to proceed with her prearranged marriage to Don Pedro.

But Bourget's interpretation focuses on the plot to the exclusion of the musical numbers, particularly the climactic "Be a Clown." Taking these into account, it is ultimately more convincing to read *The Pirate* as a self-reflexive statement, as Jane Feuer argues, about the Hollywood musical's celebration of itself as an entertainment form. Feuer sees the tendency of the classical Hollywood musical to "blow its own horn" (Feuer, 1993: 65) as being central to its ideological work. Crammed with sentiments like "Show 'em tricks, tell 'em jokes/And you'll only stop with top folks," "Be a Clown" joins such other notable rousing numbers of self-praise as "That's Entertainment" in *The Band Wagon* and "Make 'em Laugh" in *Singin' in the Rain*. In the coda of *The Pirate*, Manuela, "whose practical and dream worlds are now fused in art" (Siegel, 1971: 31), appears in full clown make-up along with Serafin for a reprise of "Be a Clown" (Plate 20). As Robin Wood explains, the utopian thrust of the musical genre informs *The Pirate*'s happy ending: the reprise is, he argues, "a celebration both of the

PLATE 20 *The Pirate*: Serafin and Manuela in the "Be a Clown" coda.

collapse of gender difference in androgyny and of the creativity that makes such a resolution possible by allowing the couple to move outside the social norms, as performers" (R. Wood, 2009: 159).

We might also consider the film as a statement by the director about the higher truth of art. "I'm an artist, not a blackmailer," as Serafin insists to Don Pedro when he pretends to be the pirate. Significantly, the various theatrical stages in the film are places where truths are revealed. As Dana Polan observes, "The stage becomes a central locus for the film as its characters find it necessary literally to stage events in order to reveal their meanings" (Polan, 2009: 136). When in Serafin's "final" performance Manuela pretends to be hypnotized, she leaves the audience and enters the theater space, now consciously performing in public. She sings "Love of My Life" to "Macoco" but really to Serafin, revealing her true feelings onstage. In this apposite "torch" song, with footlights visibly burning in the image, she intones that "now we are one," while in the choreography the two sway together, vertiginous with mutual love. Consumed with jealousy, Don Pedro rushes on stage and reveals his real identity as Macoco, whereupon he is pelted with props. Thus, "[t]heatre literally and metaphorically has destroyed the fat hypocrite" (Siegel, 1971: 31).

We may take all of this as a utopian fantasy or, as Robin Wood suggests, "an all-pervasive, precariously controlled hysteria" (R. Wood, 2009: 156), as in *Madame Bovary*. But what is finally most interesting about *The Pirate* is that it manages to offer both at once. One recalls the last lines of Keats' "Ode to a Nightingale," as the spell of the bird's beautiful song begins to fade from the narrator's consciousness: "Was it a vision, or a waking dream?" Of course, all films, on one level, are like "waking dreams," but in *The Pirate* Minnelli's extravagant visual style presents us with a film musical that is at once the waking dream of its protagonist, its audience, and its maker.

CHAPTER 6

WEST SIDE STORY (1961) AND SATURDAY NIGHT FEVER (1977)

With the exception of the genre loosely defined as folk music, the lyrics of which are often explicitly about racial discrimination, poverty, and the oppression of working people, popular music has largely avoided dealing explicitly with issues of race and class difference. The power of a song like, say, Billie Holiday's 1939 jazz vocal recording of "Strange Fruit," about the lynching of black men in the South, derives in large part precisely from its addressing a topic normally taboo in popular music. As discussed in Chapter 2, segregation and racism informed the popular music industry, including film musicals. The rare instances when a black r&b record registered enough sales to make it to the pop chart – or, vice-versa – were called crossover hits.

Both of the musicals discussed in this chapter deal with crossing over, with the difficulties arising from the attempt to transcend the differences of race and class. Both *West Side Story* and *Saturday Night Fever* are set in New York City and depict characters struggling to achieve the American Dream – a myth expressed so well in Hollywood's characteristically exuberant film musicals. Each film in its own way undermines the conventional romance plot of the classical musical to emphasize the real social problems they depict. Both shatter the utopian vision of so many of the musicals that preceded them. Indeed, so startling did the opening of *West*

The Hollywood Film Musical, First Edition. Barry Keith Grant.

Side Story seem at the time of its release that, as one reviewer rhapsodized, "the neorealist musical is about to be born" (Johnson, 1962: 59).

The plot of *West Side Story*, adapted from the popular Broadway musical, is loosely based on Shakespeare's tragedy *Romeo and Juliet*, about a pair of young "star-cross'd lovers" who choose to die because they are prevented from being together by their feuding families. Made during a period of significant Puerto Rican and Latino immigration to New York, the film transposes the action of Shakespeare's play from Verona, Italy, to contemporary New York, and changes the conflict from two warring families to tensions between white youths and recent Puerto Rican immigrants. *West Side Story* (1961) was the second highest-grossing film of the year in the United States and swept the Academy Awards, winning ten Oscars, including Best Picture – more than any other musical. It garnered uniformly enthusiastic critical accolades (with the sole exception of Pauline Kael, who in her wittily caustic review dismissed it as "a great musical for people who don't like musicals" [Kael, 1965: 146]). The soundtrack album was one of the best-selling LPs of all time up to that point.

The director, Robert Wise, began his career working at RKO as an editor, among his early assignments editing Orson Welles' *Citizen Kane* (1941) and *The Magnificent Ambersons* (1942), for which he also, uncredited, directed some additional scenes. By the time he was hired by the Mirisch Company to direct *West Side Story*, he was a seasoned director with many films to his credit. Still, although he would go on to direct *The Sound of Music* (1965) with Julie Andrews, the most commercially successful film of all time until the blockbuster movies of the 1970s, before *West Side Story* Wise had never directed a musical. Because of the director's inexperience with the genre at the time, Jerome Robbins, who choreographed and directed the stage version, was hired as co-director for the film's musical sequences. Robbins would depart from the film shortly after production began, having choreographed the opening sequence and the rumble.

Wise, like studio stalwart Howard Hawks, made films in a wide variety of genres, but for many auteurist critics, as Jean-Pierre Coursodon puts it, unlike Hawks, Wise's oeuvre exhibits "*mere* versatility; no unifying vision underlies it" (Coursodon, 1983: 368). But while this may be true of Wise's work generally, *West Side Story* nevertheless succeeds very well in translating the stage production into cinematic terms. The fact that the lead actors were chosen primarily for their physical appearance onscreen rather than for their singing abilities – indeed, most of the leads' vocals are dubbed in by other singers – suggests the attention paid to the overall design and look of the film.

Given Wise's experience as an editor, it is no surprise that *West Side Story* depends substantially on editing in the dance sequences. Indeed, the editing of these numbers, which relies heavily on montage, is noticeably different from earlier musicals, which tended to minimize editing at these points. One might argue that the editing of the dances in *West Side Story* set the stage, so to speak, for the new dance styles and their representation on film that would emerge with breakdancing and music videos two decades later. In the opening prologue dance, for example, there is an overhead shot of the Jets in a street throwing their hands up in the air followed by a cut as their hands are reaching to the basketball hoop in the schoolyard. The visibility rather than the seamlessness of the cut as it takes us from one space to another anticipates the montage construction, disruptive of the illusion of real space and time, which characterizes the music video form (Kaplan, 1987: 33ff.). The frequent editing also provides a fitting visual style to match the energy of the film's teenage characters. "You saw how they dance – like they gotta get rid of something quick. It's the same when they fight," Anita (Rita Moreno) says to Maria (Natalie Wood), speaking of the impending rumble.

As *West Side Story* begins, the musical prologue on the sound track is accompanied by an abstract image of vertical lines with changing background colors. Just as the overture introduces the musical themes to follow, so these visuals inaugurate the film's primary visual motif of entrapment. The lines then dissolve into the aerial travelling shots over Manhattan that show the tops of buildings as rigid geometric grids relieved only by the curves of highway ramps and interchanges. According to the director, this was a novel way of showing the city on film: "You were always accustomed to seeing the shot across the river and the bridge and the skyscrapers" (Kantor et al., 1970: 365). But the sequence also functions thematically, not just as an avoidance of cliché. Eventually there is a zoom combined with a dissolve that takes us to a high-angle view of an urban schoolyard with a chain-link fence surrounding it. The fence also seems to slice the space of the image down the middle so that both the kids we see playing ball and the Jets huddled in a group by the fence are forced on the left side of the frame – in cartographic terms, the west side – constrained by the environment.

The prologue dance continues to emphasize the bounded restrictions of space. As the Jets start to walk, we see them through a fence. A few shots later, Bernardo (George Chakiris) and two other Sharks walk threateningly behind two Jets, as the camera tracks along with them by shooting through the slatted siderails of a parked truck (Plate 21). This barring of the foreground is seen again when the camera tracks with the Jets from the

PLATE 21 *West Side Story:* Bernardo (George Chakiris) and his fellow Sharks in the opening sequence (Jerome Robbins and Robert Wise, 1961; Producer: Robert Wise).

interior of a construction site through the planks of hoarding. During the dance, we see one of the Jets, Baby John (Eliot Feld), painting graffiti ("Sharks stink") on a concrete wall, and suddenly the wall turns into a trap as the Sharks surround him and push him into a corner. Also, as the Jets dance, they pirouette and, turning, suddenly see Bernardo standing there, as if invading what had seemed to be their space. This pattern is repeated throughout the sequence, as various configurations of Jets or Sharks are dancing and suddenly, to their surprise as well as the viewer's, their rivals appear in the frame and momentarily threaten to disrupt the dance. One of the most startling of these moments occurs when Bernardo's hands reach into the frame and take the basketball from the Jets.

This motif graphically expresses the fear of invasion by ethnic Others that is typically generated by large waves of immigration. As the Jets agree when planning the rumble to settle the issue of turf ownership once and for all, "These PRs are different . . . They keep coming . . . Like cockroaches." They joke about "the PRs" (Puerto Ricans) coming in through the windows and taking their very air. "We fought hard for this turf and we ain't just gonna give it up," declares Riff (Russ Tamblyn), the Jets' leader. The Jets launch into "The Jet Song," which expresses their joyous feeling of community in being part of the pack ("Without a gang you're an orphan," Riff later tells Tony) and also defines their group in exclusionary terms ("every Puerto Rican's a lousy chicken"). During the war council in Doc's candy store, Riff tells Bernardo, "You crossed the line once too often," making explicit the link between the constrained space of the mise-en-scène and the prison of prejudice that fuels the behavior of both groups of teenagers, and which, in the end, will prove to be, in Shakespeare's words, a plague on both their houses.

The entrapping design of the mise-en-scène continues throughout the film. During the novelty number "Gee, Officer Krupke," for example, Riff gestures spastically, a victim of his upbringing (referred to in the song as a "social disease"), from behind improvised prison bars as Action (Tony Mordente), mocking social workers, sings that Riff "needs a year in the pen." When Tony (Richard Beymer) reveals to Doc (Ned Glass) that he is in love with a Puerto Rican girl, Doc says he's afraid for both of them, the reinforced door of his store casting a grid of shadows across his face. At the rumble, the Sharks have to climb over a chain-link fence to get in to the space where both gangs have agreed to fight, while the Jets come through a similar fence on the opposite side. They line up along the fence and then clamber down a concrete wall, reversing this when they flee the scene as the police sirens begin to wail. As the fight begins, Riff is pushed up against a fence, his arms spread in a Christ-like way, suggesting the sacrificial nature of his imminent death and that these young people need forgiveness because they know not what they do.

When Tony sings "Something's Coming," he is in the narrow confines of an alley behind Doc's candy store, the brick walls seeming to press in on him. There is a stair railing to Tony's right and a fire escape above him on the left. Only a little patch of sky is visible between the buildings beyond the clotheslines of washing hanging from windows. Escape from this place cannot be easy, and the song's lyrics also pick up on the motif, as Tony sings that one day "the phone will jingle, the door will knock/Open the latch." The metaphor of opening up a previously locked door as a result of social connection suggests the potential solution for the film's characters, now trapped by their own racist fears. Just before the fight breaks out in the prologue, Baby John is chased beside a makeshift wall comprised entirely of old doors. Later, in the "America" number, Bernardo counters Anita's optimism in one verse ("lots of new housing with more space") with "Lots of doors slamming in our face." Hearing mention of Maria for the first time, an enchanted Tony leaves the gym singing the famous song bearing her name, and when he reaches the part where he chants it over and over, he comes to that fence in the schoolyard – but now the gates are flung open for him, and he bursts through them in song. We suddenly see him in front of a series of stained-glass windows, presumably a church, as he concludes that her name "is almost like praying."

On the fire escape in the film's version of Shakespeare's balcony scene, Maria tells Tony that they belong to mutually exclusive communities ("you're not one of us and I'm not one of you") (Plate 22). The racist attitudes in the world of the West Side are firmly entrenched, and the bars of the fire escape foreshadow the young lovers' fate. As they part, Maria is behind the bars holding them, while Tony is behind them on the other side, with the steps of the fire escape bifurcating the image and separating them. Earlier, in "I Feel Pretty," sung in the grip of her first flush of love, Maria is costumed to evoke the Statue of Liberty. She is one of the "huddled masses yearning to breathe free." But on the fire escape, the bars of the steps that shutter Tony as he declares his love suggest that, in a racially divided America, interracial romance is doomed. Later, when Maria hears what has happened at the rumble, she runs after Chino (Jose De Vega) down a stairway shown from a high angle as if it were an entrapping maze, and when Tony thinks Maria is dead, he is shown pressing against a chain-link fence in despair.

After learning of her boyfriend Bernardo's death at the hand of Tony, Anita sings vehemently to Maria, "One of your own kind, stick to your own kind." The percussive and staccato effects of the musical arrangement here reinforce the seemingly inviolable boundaries between the two cultures. But when Tony and Maria perform "Tonight," initially they sing in turn, individually, and in counterpoint, then together and in harmony, the change in the musical arrangement here expressing their shared wish to transcend the animosity that fuels both groups. When the two first meet at the gym and, immediately enchanted by each other, begin to dance, the musical arrangement becomes lighter, with high notes of piccolos, and their arms are held akimbo; it is as if they are walking on air, rising above the prejudice that entraps everyone living on the West Side. Later, the couple imagine getting away, fleeing their world, and then, as they kiss after singing "Somewhere," they embrace and disappear below the bottom of the frame, reversing the numerous intrusions into the frame during the prologue, as discussed above, and suggesting that the only place they could be together in peace is out of this world.

The barriers between the two cultures are also expressed in the film's music, particularly in its opposition of mambo and jazz. Jazz, often described as an American musical invention, is associated with the Jets.

PLATE 22 *West Side Story*: Maria (Natalie Wood) and Tony (Richard Beymer) on the fire escape.

The jazz influence is perhaps most overt in "Cool," sung by Ice (Tucker Smith), a character created for the film, and danced by the Jets after the rumble. Elmer Bernstein's music employs elements of modern or cool jazz in its composition and arrangement, and Stephen Sondheim's lyrics pick up on the slang associated with it, in the song's title, obviously, and in the lyrics

("Daddy-O," "Go, man, go"), as well as in Ice's segue into the song, warning the gang that "you all better dig this and dig this good." Significantly, when Riff asks Bernardo to meet him later at Doc's for the war council, he warns him, "And no jazz before then." By contrast, while the Jets are associated with cool jazz, the Sharks are associated with the more sensual, or "hotter," Latin musical styles of mambo and flamenco. Mambo was brought to New York from Cuba and popularized by Perez Prado, the first musician to market his music as "mambo," in the late 1940s and early 1950s, while flamenco originated in Spain but includes musical elements brought back from the Americas during the nation's colonial period. Unlike the Jets, the Sharks and their girlfriends begin dancing at the gym with a mambo, and when Anita goes to Doc's to warn Tony and the Jets taunt her with racial insults before attempting to rape her, mambo plays on the candy store jukebox. During the "America" number on the roof, the Puerto Ricans inflect their dancing with flamenco steps, but also other dance styles to reflect at once their own identity and the American melting pot that the women invoke so positively in the song's lyrics (Plate 23).

PLATE 23 *West Side Story*: Anita (Rita Moreno) defends the mythic melting pot of "America" compared to the conditions in Puerto Rico.

As the Jets molest Anita, who has come to Doc's to deliver Maria's message to Tony, and they force Baby John on top of her, a few notes of "America" interpellated in the music signal a wider critique within *West Side Story*'s tragic narrative. While the Puerto Ricans dance in the "America" number, the choreography pointedly includes a mime slap-down to coincide with the word "America." Indeed, one cannot easily refute Bernardo's claims about racial injustice during the number, when he observes that a white boy would make twice as much as Chino for doing the same job. The clearly biased detective Lt Schrank (Simon Oakland) indicates the institutionalization of racism and hence the truth of Bernardo's observation. Barely hiding his disgust at the immigrant invaders, Schrank, the representative of law and justice, treats the Jets and Sharks differently, ordering the Sharks out of the schoolyard or candy store and then trying to reason with the white boys.

When a disgusted Doc breaks up the assault on Anita and asks, "When do you kids stop? You make this world lousy," Action quickly retorts, "We didn't make it, Doc." This general condemnation is given added poignancy by the location of the rumble below a highway overpass, as it is the middle class, those who can afford automobiles, who are driving by above, oblivious to this hellish world seething below them. In the climax in the schoolyard, after Chino shoots Tony, Maria utters the final withering truth as both gangs, in shared guilt, lift up Tony's body to carry him away: "All of you, you all killed him . . . not with bullets and guns, but with hate."

In the impossibly harmonious place Tony and Maria musically fantasize in "Somewhere," they sing "hold my hand and we're halfway there . . . ." This halfway point is as far as the Tony of *Saturday Night Fever* manages to escape from his world. Tony Manero (John Travolta) struggles in the film to transcend the stereotypes that inform the worldview of his working-class Italian neighborhood of Bay Ridge, Brooklyn. In the film's final shots, when he makes the decision to leave Bay Ridge and the disco scene behind, he holds hands with and then is hugged by Stephanie (Karen Lynn Gorney). While the film seems to celebrate the disco scene, in fact in the end, unlike many classical musicals, it rejects the myth of dance's transformative power.

Saturday Night Fever was released during the disco dance fad of the late 1970s and helped significantly in popularizing it. The soundtrack LP, featuring the music of the Bee Gees as well as Walter Murphy, Yvonne Elliman, and KC and the Sunshine Band, among other disco stars, contained several no. 1 hits and was one of the best-selling soundtrack albums of all time, reportedly selling over 12 million copies (Shaw, 1982: 106). The film spawned a cycle of other disco movies, including *Thank God It's Friday* (1978), *Roller Boogie* (1979), *Xanadu* (1980), *Can't Stop the Music* (1980), and *Fame* (1980), as well as *Saturday Night Fever*'s less successful sequel, *Staying Alive* (1983), which showed Tony five years later trying to succeed as a dancer on Broadway. The original version of *Saturday Night Fever* (the one considered here) was R-rated, but was re-released the year after its successful first run in a recut PG-rated version that eliminated the nudity, the rape scene, drug use, and much of the profanity.

In 1976, the year before the film's release, pop music critic Nik Cohn published a *New York* magazine cover story, "Tribal Rites of the New Saturday Night," which was used as the basis for the film by screenwriter Norman Wexler, who wrote the screenplays for *Joe* (1969) and *Serpico* (1973), both of which also explore characters trapped and shaped by the urban environment of New York City. For Travolta, who had made an impression as Vinnie Barbarino in the popular television sitcom *Welcome Back, Kotter* (1975–9), it was his first starring role in a theatrical film, although he already had appeared in a small part in Brian De Palma's cult horror film *Carrie*, and had starred in the TV movie *The Boy in the Plastic Bubble* (both 1976). Travolta's impressive dancing in *Saturday Night Fever* helped him get his next starring role as Danny Zuko in the movie version of *Grease* (1978), opposite pop star Olivia Newton-John in her unmemorable screen debut. John Avildsen, the director of *Joe*, was originally lined up to direct *Saturday Night Fever*, but then dropped out, to be replaced by John Badham, who had only one other feature film to his credit at the time – *The Bingo Long Traveling All-Stars & Motor Kings* (1976), about the defunct Negro baseball league. Badham has made no other musicals, and since the late 1990s has worked primarily in television, where he began his career.

With its pulsating lights, redundant and simple rhythms, sweetened use of strings, minimal lyrical content, and emphasis on fashion ("Polyester on a dance floor? He's a creep," pronounces one disco girl in *Thank God It's Friday*), the disco experience denied the pressing realities of the real world outside by creating a seductively enclosed environment, a pleasure dome, which served as a We're-in-the-Money fantasy for post-Baby Boomer youth. The repetitiveness and shallowness of the music were held in suspicion by many "authentic" rockers, who considered the style anti-thetical to, indeed a betrayal of, "real" rock 'n' roll. Unlike earlier rock music, disco's musical style encouraged the sublimation of desire – "rushes and flashes instead of feeling and reeling," in the contemptuous words of Frank Zappa (Zappa, 1970: 44), who also recorded the satiric song "Disco Boy" (1976). Disco became the object of a marketing frenzy, with many musicals artists abandoning their distinctive style to make frankly execrable disco records, from Broadway vocalists such as Ethel Merman and Barbra Streisand to jazz artists including keyboardist Herbie Hancock and flautist Herbie Mann. (Not coincidentally, one of these musical artists, Monti Rock, who reinvented himself in the disco era as the equally talentless Disco Tex, plays Monte, the disc jockey at the 2001 Odyssey in *Saturday Night Fever*.) In due course, a backlash arose against disco as shallow and soulless, which culminated in an anti-disco "riot" after a Chicago White Sox baseball game at Comiskey Park on July 12, 1979. A promotional event dubbed "Disco Demolition Night" that drew an unexpectedly large crowd estimated as high as 90,000, it began with piles of disco records burned on the infield, then followed by fans pouring from the stands onto the field and destroying it.

Almost alone in articulating a defense of disco, Richard Dyer argued that, rather than a vapid form of popular music, it had important aesthetic and ideological value because its dances generated what he called a "whole body" eroticism. Disco dancing, he noted, "restores eroticism to the whole of the body and for both sexes, not just confining it to the penis. It leads to the expressive, sinuous movement of disco dancing, not just that mixture of awkwardness and thrust so dismally characteristic of dancing to rock" (Dyer, 1990: 13, 15). Disco, for Dyer, presented a challenge to the otherwise pervasive and aggressive phallicism of rock music.

Interestingly, *Saturday Night Fever* shows us both aspects of disco. The movie manages to expose the shallow pleasures of the disco scene even as it works to provide the audience with its pleasures, primarily in Tony's dancing. For Pauline Kael, as for many reviewers, "[t]hese are among the most hypnotically beautiful pop dance scenes ever filmed" (Kael, 1980: 368). Yet at the same time, the film follows Tony's journey of personal growth in which he comes to understand that disco dancing is not an alternative to or an escape from the real world. It is no coincidence that as the film moves toward its climax, as Tony begins to comprehend the limitations of his world and so desires to change, it abandons the music to concentrate instead on its dramatic narrative.

Like *West Side Story*, *Saturday Night Fever* begins with aerial shots of New York City, before panning to a particular neighborhood, to emphasize its restrictive nature. Just before the Bee Gees' catchy "Stayin' Alive" begins, the camera takes us from above the elevated subway to below it – to street level, the mundane reality where Tony dwells during the day and from which he lifts off on weekend nights to the heights of greatness at the 2001 Odyssey. The name of the discothèque, referring to Stanley Kubrick's famous 1968 science fiction film, points to Tony's attempt to transcend the limitations of his world, just as in Kubrick's movie the astronaut Bowman (Keir Dullea) is propelled into the Stargate, a space of expanded consciousness and potential. On the ground, Tony is oppressed at home by bickering and unsupportive parents and on the street by his loutish teenage friends. His boss in the paint and hardware store where he works offers him job security by reminding him that another employee has been with him for fifteen years, but Tony sees this only as sealing a dead-end fate. In his room, posters of Al Pacino and Sylvester Stallone (who, coincidentally, would direct the sequel, *Staying Alive*), Italian-Americans from New York who have made it big in the entertainment industry, reflect Tony's aspirations for success and his yearning to escape his narrow world.

On weekend nights, Tony dons his disco duds and heads to the 2001 Odyssey, where he is no longer a mere sales clerk, and, like Bowman reborn as the Star Child in Kubrick's film, is transformed into somebody better. Everyone seems to know Tony, and when he dances he reigns on the dance floor (another dancer refers to him explicitly as king), the crowd moving aside to watch. Just as in *Rocky* (1976) Stallone's boxer had run up the steps of the Philadelphia Museum of Art, inspired that he's "gonna fly now," so Tony's dancing at the disco temporarily allows him to rise above his daily cares – at least until he begins to have deeper ambitions. The disco is a heavenly world, complete with electric stars twinkling around the colorfully flashing floor as the crowd dances to Walter Murphy's "A Fifth of Beethoven." Even the pinnacle of Western classical music can be transformed by disco. Close-ups of swirling hips and flashing lights emphasize the allure of the disco world (his brother Frank Jr [Martin Shakar] clearly uncomfortable there, tells Tony that the place is "energizing"). When, later, Tony is put off by his friends' typically impersonal approach to having sex with girls in the back seat of their car, he promptly turns away and re-enters the comforting sanctuary of the discothèque. Here he joins in a line dance to the Bee Gees' "Night Fever" as all the dancers on the floor know the steps and move together in an idyllic community.

The scenes of the Manero family at the dinner table stand in stark contrast to the harmony of the disco. At the table, Tony wears a bedsheet around him to protect his disco outfit from being splashed with spaghetti sauce, but it also suggests the self-defensive armor that he must deploy to survive at home, where his family routinely shout at and slap each other. It is not difficult to see why, for Tony, the worshipful congregation of dancers at the disco takes the place of religion for him. After leaving the Church and moving on with his life, his brother, Frank Jr leaves his clerical collar as a parting gift for Tony, who pretends to hang himself with it in the mirror. By contrast, a montage of Tony dressing for a night at the disco depicts it as a solemn ritual: his puts on his clothes and gold chains – including, notably, a crucifix – as if he were donning sacred vestments. When Tony takes Frank Jr to the disco, Frank observes to his brother, "You arrive, and the crowd parts like the Red Sea."

The importance of this metaphor is picked up in the film's recurrent bridge imagery. The first shot of the film is of the Brooklyn Bridge, the second of the Verazzano-Narrows Bridge, which connects Brooklyn and Staten Island, with the Manhattan skyline visible in the far distance. This bridge looms in the background of several scenes, and is crucial at several points in the narrative. When Tony and his friends go on the bridge, the accompanying music is David Shire's "Night on Disco Mountain," a disco adaptation of Mussorgsky's melodramatic "Night on Bald Mountain," underscoring its monumental presence. Ultimately, the Bridge functions in the film not just as an architectural span connecting two boroughs of New York City, but as a metaphor for potential change. When he first goes out for coffee with Stephanie, who represents this wider world for Tony, the Bridge is visible behind them, at the end of the street. She comments that although Manhattan is just across the river it seems like a totally different world. Later, when Tony tells an upset Stephanie some facts about it ("I know everything about that bridge"), they share their first intimate moment together as she hesitantly touches his cheek. By contrast, Tony's friends engage in childish horseplay on its cables and catwalks, revealing their inability to cross this bridge when they come to it, while Bobby C (Barry Miller), who cannot cope with facing up to his responsibilities and marrying his pregnant girlfriend, later falls to his death from it. The Bridge spans the Narrows, which separates the smaller upper bay at the mouth of the Hudson River from the larger lower bay, and so perhaps it also mirrors Tony's dawning struggle to transform from a big fish in a small pond to a small one in a bigger sea.

From the very beginning the film shows Tony's struggle. As the Bee Gees sing "Stayin' Alive" in the film's famous opening number, we see images of Tony swaggering down the street. (In contrast, Bobby C, on whom platform shoes seem merely silly, describes himself as "paralyzed" before he falls from the bridge.) The camera tracks low to the ground, retreating from the steady advance of Tony's shoes as he struts as if in rhythm with the Bee Gees' non-diegetic tune. (Ironically, Travolta was not available when this scene was shot, so the close-ups of Tony's boots as he walks are actually the feet of a stand-in.) In the opening number, a full shot on the street shows people shambling about their business, each with his or her own rhythm, though perhaps not as brash as Tony's. Yet although Tony acts as if he's got "the wings of heaven" on his shoes and is "a dancin' man" who "just can't lose," as the Bee Gees sing, this may be just a mask covering his insecurity, one that already begins to crack as he swaggers by an attractive woman with a walk as rhythmical as his, but whose look makes it clear that she doesn't have the time of day for him. The sequence ends as Tony returns to work through the back door of the store, then overcharges a waiting customer by several dollars for a can of paint that he had just bought from another retailer but charming her nonetheless by offering her a dollar discount for her patience. "Feel the city breakin'/And everybody shakin'," trying to stay alive, as the Bee Gees sing.

At the beginning, Tony dismisses his boss's advice about planning his life by snapping "Fuck the future"; but he begins to see beyond the immediate pleasures of the disco when he first spots Stephanie there one night. The lyrics of the Bee Gees' "Night Fever" indicate his immediate infatuation with her: "And that sweet city woman/She moves through the light/ Controlling my mind and my soul." As a result, Tony decides to dance with her instead of Annette (Donna Pescow), a doting neighborhood girl who has been his dance partner before. When he first encounters Stephanie at the dance studio, she is practicing ballet to classical piano music – appropriately highbrow, for as a career girl she represents the possibility of upwardly mobile success for Tony. Visually, the horizontal ballet bar she holds onto offers a graphic contrast to the vertical pole around which the stripper dances at the discothèque. At their first rehearsal, they dance to Tavares' "More Than a Woman," its title refrain speaking to the symbolic importance Stephanie represents for Tony. They quickly move from a smaller rehearsal room to the largest dance floor in the studio, its bigger size indicative of the new horizons Tony is beginning to glimpse. They proceed to show each other some steps, a dialogue in dance of equal partners, and then they dance the Latin Hustle together, dancing perfectly in step like Astaire and Rogers (Plate 24). Well, perhaps not quite like Astaire and Rogers: criticism of the film has frequently focused on Karen Lynn Gorney's decidedly mediocre dancing ability, despite Tony's judgment of her skill. But this discrepancy is actually to the point since it suggests that Tony is so desperate to leave Bay Ridge behind that he may be blind to reality.

Despite her initial resistance, Tony convinces Stephanie to be his partner for the upcoming big dance contest. At the contest, they are preceded by a black couple and followed by a Latino couple, both of whom dance with considerably more energy. Indeed, Tony and Stephanie forget about their dance to "More Than a Woman," and slowly embrace and then kiss, lost in the mutual attraction of the moment (Plate 25).

PLATE 24 *Saturday Night Fever:* Tony Manero (John Travolta) and Stephanie (Karen Lynn Gorney) in a relaxed moment during rehearsal (John Badham, 1977; Producer: Robert Stigwood).

PLATE 25 *Saturday Night Fever:* Tony and Stephanie on the seductive dance floor at the 2001 Odyssey discothèque.

Nevertheless, they win the dance contest, but for Tony it is a hollow victory: he realizes that the Latino couple were better, and that they lost only because of the pervasive racism in Bay Ridge. As one of Tony's friends says when Tony watches the Latino couple admiringly, "What do you expect? They're Spics – look at them greasin' up the floor."

In Tony's world, whiteness (not to mention patriarchy) is the center from which others are marginalized, as is clear almost from the beginning. After "Stayin' Alive," he jokes with his second customer, who complains about his impending paint job by remarking that he would like to paint his wife's ass purple. When Tony asks "What color is her ass now?" the customer replies that "actually, it's ain't got no color," indicating that from their mutual perspective white is not a color, but its absence. That night, arriving at the 2001 Odyssey, Tony and his friends make racist comments about the way the black and Latino dancers dress. And later, when one of their buddies, Gus (Bruce Ornstein), is hospitalized after being jumped, Tony and his friends Double J (Paul Pape) and Joey (Joseph Cali) seek revenge by smashing Bobby C's car through the window of the hangout of a local Puerto Rican gang, the Barracudas, only to find out later from Gus that they may not have been the ones responsible for beating him.

Realizing the racism involved in judging the contest, Tony gives the first-place prize and trophy to the Latino couple, apparently renouncing the disco scene as he leaves in disgust. As he does so, there is a brief reprise of "Stayin' Alive" on the sound track, and although the Bee Gees sing "it's all right, it's OK/And you may look the other way," Tony is unable to turn a blind eye. Now he regards the 2001 Odyssey as a "shithole," and shortly after, he tells the detective investigating whether Bobby C might have committed suicide, "There are ways of killin' yourself without killin' yourself." Leaving his friends behind, Tony spends his dark night of the soul riding the subway, a journey that is also a burrowing within, into the self. Significantly, the song played at this point is the Bee Gees' "How Deep is Your Love." As a result of his soul searching, Tony makes his crucial decision. In the morning light of a new day, he comes to Stephanie's apartment in Manhattan – another world, as she had described it – his soiled white disco suit suggesting the battering of his earlier worldview. The wounds on his face from the gang fight serve as "red badges of courage" of the personal battle he has been waging to wrestle himself free of Bay Ridge's "dog-eat-dog" philosophy. When Double J and Joey espouse this bleak view of social relations while they cruise in Bobby C's car, there is a pensive close-up of Tony which dissolves to a paint can being shaken by the mixing machine in the store where he works. Like that can of paint, Tony has been irreversibly shaken. "Listen to the ground/There is movement all around/. . . And I can feel it," as the Bee Gees sing in "Night Fever." The "bridge" to a new and better life happens for Tony underground, in the dark tunnels of the subway.

Apologizing to Stephanie for his earlier behavior in trying to force himself on her, Tony tells her that he has made the decision to leave Brooklyn behind and move to Manhattan. All along she has rebuffed his sexual advances, and now Tony says he wants just to be friends, but admits that he doesn't know how to with women, who are little more than sex objects for his peer group. Sympathetic to his wish to free himself from the shackles of his upbringing, Stephanie takes his hand in hers, and then in the final image they hug. As they do, behind them in this last scene is a large window looking outside to a Manhattan street, the new and difficult world that will possibly open up to Tony.

Dance in *Saturday Night Fever*, then, does not possess the transformative power of earlier musicals. It cannot move beyond the four walls of the discothèque, where it's more a matter of stayin' alive than of simply putting a shine on one's shoes. The film's plot gestures toward the romantic conflicts of earlier musicals, generating the expectation that, as in the Astaire–Rogers movies, when the couple dance together (and here, even rapturously kiss) their romantic union will follow soon thereafter. While Fred and Ginger may shake hands after dancing "It's a Lovely Day" in *Top Hat* (1935), it is only a step toward their more perfectly romantic union. But *Saturday Night Fever* ends with Tony and Stephanie shaking hands as a gesture of friendship rather than romance. Their handshake at once counters the basically solipsistic dance style of disco and realizes the potential for friendship that "bridges" individual existence. Kael complained that the boy-meets-girl ending of *Saturday Night Fever* "doesn't feel as up as it should" (Kael, 1980: 371), but this is precisely the point of the film. As one critic has argued, *Saturday Night Fever* is "about surviving with integrity and emotional sensitivity in sub- and larger cultures where glittery shams demand that one sacrifice both integrity and sensitivity to win dubious rewards" (Hasbany, 1978: 562). This, according to the film, is what the battle of "stayin' alive" is all about.

CHAPTER 7

WOODSTOCK (1970)

Woodstock celebrates the now legendary Woodstock Music and Art Fair ("An Aquarian Exposition: three days of peace & music") held at Max Yasgur's 600-acre farm in the town of Bethel near Woodstock, New York, from August 15 to 18, 1969. Attended by an unexpectedly large crowd of close to half a million people, the Festival transpired peacefully despite inadequate toilet facilities, insufficient supplies, and a rainstorm that turned the fields into muddy bogs. The peaceful Festival was regarded as the pinnacle of the hippie movement (immortalized in Joni Mitchell's song "Woodstock," although she herself chose not to attend). Generally acknowledged as the mother of all rockumentaries – for one critic, "a super sixties New Generation MGM musical with enough climaxes to wear out Masters and Johnson" (Fuller, 1972: 74) – *Woodstock* not only is a chronicle of this iconic concert, but also aims to be a contemporary cultural statement like the music it documents. The film depicts the Woodstock event as a harmonious counter-cultural commune (the "Woodstock nation," as it has since been called) unfolding in the bucolic fields of Yazgur's farmland that fulfills the utopian ideals of the musical genre.

Woodstock was made for Warner Bros, which, with a new regime under Ted Ashley, was moving in the direction of making "hipper" films for a growing youth culture that was receptive to the experimentation of European art cinema. Over the objections of other studio executives, the film was produced by Fred Weintraub, one of Ashley's hires who also

The Hollywood Film Musical, First Edition. Barry Keith Grant.
© 2012 Barry Keith Grant. Published 2012 by Blackwell Publishing Ltd.

owned the Bitter End Coffeehouse in Greenwich Village. Artie Kornfeld, a songwriter and vice-president of Capitol Records and one of the four producers of the Woodstock concert, approached Weintraub for money to make the film, and, in the face of some resistance, the latter was able to provide the rather small sum of $100,000 necessary. Upon its initial release in 1970, *Woodstock* would earn $16.4 million in domestic rentals alone, win the Oscar for Best Documentary Feature, and help save Warner Bros from bankruptcy (Biskind, 1998: 85).

Originally shot on 16 mm and then blown up to the standard 35 mm for theatrical release, *Woodstock* was edited from more than 1,210 hours of footage. Six editors, including future director Martin Scorsese, and nine editorial assistants cut the film. Thelma Schoonmaker, who was nominated for an Oscar for Film Editing, would go on to edit numerous films for Scorsese. *Woodstock* was directed by Michael Wadleigh, who also served as one of the film's five principal cinematographers (seven others are also credited). Years later, Wadleigh also used footage shot at the concert to make *Woodstock: The Lost Performances* (1990) and *Jimi Hendrix: Live at Woodstock* (1999). Wadleigh's one venture into fiction filmmaking, *Wolfen* (1981), brought something of a similar counter-cultural sensibility to the horror genre, with its indigenous American shapeshifters who stalk the South Bronx as a result of being displaced by advancing civilization. Documentary films also have been made about the follow-up Woodstock concerts in 1994 and 1999, the most interesting of which is Barbara Kopple's *My Generation* (2000), which contrasts all three events and focuses on the changing motivations and values that informed each of them.

The Official Director's Cut of *Woodstock* (subtitled *3 Days of Peace & Music*), which added forty minutes of new material for a total running time of almost four hours, was released in 1994. In this expanded version, the one most widely available and the one on which the discussion in this chapter is based, Wadleigh replaced some of the crowd scenes in the original film with previously unseen footage. Both the original film and the Director's Cut shuffle the actual order of performances at the Festival, although in both cases the opening and closing acts (Richie Havens and Jimi Hendrix, respectively) are the same as they were at the actual concert. Among the thirty-two acts that performed over the four days and whose performances are captured in the film are Crosby, Stills and Nash, Richie Havens, Joan Baez, The Who, Sha-Na-Na, Joe Cocker, Country Joe and the Fish, and Arlo Guthrie; artists who performed at Woodstock but did not appear in the original film include The Incredible String Band, Ravi Shankar, Melanie, The Band, Blood Sweat & Tears, Johnny and Edgar Winter, Paul Butterfield, The Grateful Dead, Creedence Clearwater

Revival, Jefferson Airplane, Canned Heat, and Janis Joplin, although the latter three are in the Director's Cut. (In 2009 a remastered fortieth anniversary DVD edition, which added two further hours of previously unseen performance footage, was released.)

Every documentary is a constructed representation of the event it depicts: choices are made about what to film, what footage to use or exclude, and how to organize it. In *Woodstock* specifically, decisions were made about which artists and which songs from their sets to include, and where to place shots within sequences and sequences within the film. It is hardly what it might appear at first sight: a random accumulation of performance footage, scenes of concertgoers listening, dancing, smoking marijuana, and swimming in the nude, and interviews with organizers, local townspeople, and fans. Initially, the film appears to be an assemblage of scenes simply intended to immerse viewers in the overwhelming experience of the event; but, as one of the film's cameramen tells a man he is interviewing by the portable toilets, the film is only "partly" about the Festival.

By the end of the 1960s, the developing "counter-culture" had had a profound impact on popular music. In the film, Mike Lang, co-producer of the Festival, says the music is "about what's happening now," and that if you listen to the music and the lyrics, "then you'll know what's going on in the culture." One only has to listen to the music in the influential youth-biker-road movie *Easy Rider* (1969), herald of a new wave of counter-cultural youth films in the early 1970s, to understand how the rock music of the time expressed what Richard Goldstein then called "the sacred squeal of now" (Goldstein, 1969: 11). In *Woodstock*, this "sacred squeal" is the musical expression of the counter-culture's rejection of middle-class values and lifestyle in favor of a more open and accepting society.

In *The Last Waltz* (1978), the acclaimed documentary about the final concert by The Band, Martin Scorsese ignores the audience almost entirely (on occasion one may glimpse hands reaching toward the stage from a lower corner of the frame); instead, he chooses to emphasize the group as a self-contained entity who play together in tight harmony, exactly what they were known for. In addition, the film's frequent use of rack focus, subtly shifting the visual emphasis from one member of the band to another as the depth of field within shots changes during performances, graphically visualizes the musical dialogue taking place between the musicians. *Woodstock*, by contrast, features peripatetic cameras that constantly move about, mixing the performances on stage with shots of the people at the historic concert, to convey the idea that the audience has been brought together through the music. In Ang Lee's *Taking Woodstock* (2009), based on the memoir by Elliott Tiber, who provided the concert permit to Mike Lang, during the concert Elliott (Demetri Martin) looks from a hilltop to the stage in the distance with the immense crowd around it and, under the influence of LSD, experiences it as undulating waves, like one mighty organic creature grooving to the pulsing music. The same idea informs *Woodstock*: it's a backstage musical in which everyone in the audience, not just the performers, is part of putting on the show. Indeed, in this film they *are* the show (Plate 26).

Most obviously, of course, much of the music, and the manner in which it is performed, despite the incredibly diverse styles of the various performers, relates to the theme of community. The first artist we see, Richie Havens, gets everyone to clap in time while performing "Motherless Child," thus making his performance interactive. A cutaway shows everyone rising and clapping, starting by focusing on a small group and then zooming out to take in a sea of people filling the entire frame. At one point Havens says the concert is more about "you," the people out there listening, than the music alone. Sly Stewart of Sly and the Family Stone also invites the audience to interact, to become part of the performance of "I Want to Take You Higher," by telling them that sing-alongs are not "old-fashioned" (Plate 27). Sly and the Family Stone was the first group composed of both male and female and black and white performers, the band's diverse membership itself signifying the musical

PLATE 26 *Woodstock*: The audience becomes the show at the famous music festival (Michael Wadleigh, 1970; Producer: Bob Maurice).

PLATE 27 *Woodstock*: Sly Stone encourages the audience to join in.

utopia of Woodstock. During Canned Heat's performance of "A Change is Gonna Come," a fan comes up on stage and mooches a cigarette from singer Bob Hite, the song continuing without missing a beat. Another form of musical interactivity occurs when Pete Townsend of The Who smashes his guitar and tosses it out into the audience upon completion of the band's set. Off the stage, among the shots of people at the Festival we see a group of nude swimmers singing "Row, Row, Row Your Boat," their physical proximity miming being in a boat and their musical round of overlapping vocal lines adding to the expression of music as social harmony. All of this suggests that, like smiling in Crosby, Stills and Nash's "Wooden Ships," music is something people understand "'Cause that is something everyone everywhere does in the same language."

Crosby, Stills and Nash's "Long Time Comin'" (the first song we hear in the film, but actually performed on Saturday, the second day) accompanies a montage that shows the building of the stage through the gradual appearance of machinery on the lovely rural landscape. A long shot of this pastoral setting shows the stage being built, small enough in the picture not to seem too intrusive. A dozen workers together hoist a huge frame into place, like a traditional community barn-raising. A 360-degree pan shot reinforces the sense of a group working toward a common goal. (Contrastingly, at one point in the song, as the trio sing "you've got to speak out against the madness," there is a shot with barbed wire in the foreground, the image connoting containment and restriction and associating it with society at large.) Some of the shots are from a low angle, at the level of grass and goldenrod, implying the closeness to nature that informed the counter-culture (Roszak, 1969) and that also characterizes the film's view of the entire event – getting back to the garden, to quote Joni Mitchell's title song. The sequence ends with "Long Time Comin'" fading out on the soundtrack as a spotlight is being hoisted high up in the air for placement on one of the towers flanking the stage. The image foreshadows both Joe Cocker singing that "I get high with a little help from my friends" and Sly and the Family Stone urging "I want to take you higher" – both songs emphasizing positive interaction – and metaphorically represents the lofty social idealism of the Woodstock participants. As Cocker says by way of introducing "With a Little Help from My Friends," "this title just about puts it all into focus."

The second song in the film, Canned Heat's "Going Up the Country," is likewise thematically crucial, although again we do not see the group perform it. Instead, a studio recording of the song is accompanied by a thematically linked montage sequence of fans at the Festival. Jim Horn's prominent flute in the band's arrangement of this 1920s blues song – an unusual instrument in blues of any era – suggests a sense of escape, of unburdening oneself of materialism and responsibility, promised by leaving the city. The song's lyrics, in which the singer bemoans the fact that with "all this fussin' and fightin', man, you know I sure can't stay/ . . . might even leave the USA," reinforce this idea. The song's view of dropping out as social protest suggests a shared rejection of certain bourgeois values that unites the members of the Woodstock community, consistent with Theodore Roszak's discussion of the counter-culture's rejection of urban materialism (Roszak, 1969). The point is emphasized by the long take that begins on the line "I've got to leave the city," with the camera panning across many of the listening fans' faces. The long take, preserving space and time, further connects all the Woodstock attendees by keeping them in the same shot. When the camera captures a debate between two men, one clean-cut and one a hippie, about the semantics of the word "freak," the camera swings around to include an American flag on a pole behind the latter: this disagreement represents nothing less than the generation gap that was separating Americans across the country.

The montage accompanying the Canned Heat song shows groups of hippies arriving in school buses, some dressed with outrageous feathers in their hair. The feathers recall the first shot of the sequence, which shows several people standing around a tepee, associating them with Native Americans, marginalized and oppressed peoples who resisted dominant culture (the advance of "civilization"). It is no surprise that the western genre suffered both substantial revision and a serious decline in popularity during this time. Yet other people are seen walking with backpacks and guitars – goin' up the country as a pilgrimage to share in the communal enjoyment of music making. There are pregnant women and children, and even three nuns, one of whom, as they walk past the camera, flashes the peace sign. (The shot is amusingly re-created in *Taking Woodstock* when we see the filmmakers talk the nuns into doing it.) The film briefly freezes the image of the nun's gesture, emphasizing that the peace movement is not confined solely to these self-described "freaks." Shots of people dancing and gyrating, shown as silhouettes against the gathering night, are but the film's first suggestion of the Woodstock community as a tribal ritual. The cut from the shot of a man dancing in silhouette to a matching shot of a child dancing offers the idea that the Woodstock participants are wonderfully innocent and idealistic youths rather than threatening in their alternate lifestyle. The sequence ends with a fadeout from the image of a child dancing in the night.

Like the song they play, Canned Heat's name was taken from a classic blues tune (Tommy Johnson's 1928 "Canned Heat Blues"). The blues, a musical form developed by black musicians in the South, experienced a revival with young white audiences in the 1960s, who identified with the social oppression it expressed. Because of its open acknowledgment of sexuality, the blues was also regarded as "counter" to the romantic clichés of mainstream popular music. The lyrics of blues songs tended to work against the conventions of the songs churned out by Tin Pan Alley and Brill Building Pop, which were seen in comparison as formulaic and inauthentic insofar as they expressed a romantic and sublimated love vision that did not square with the courting rituals and sexual realities of a generation embracing the new ideology of "free love." Thus there are several blues-based tunes in *Woodstock* in addition to Canned Heat's "Goin' Up the Country," including The Who's version of Eddie Cochran's 1958 hit "Summertime Blues," Jefferson Airplane's "Uncle Sam's Blues," and Ten Years After's "I'm Going Home."

The film in part builds its sense of community through a resistance to the Vietnam War specifically, a view shared by both musicians and fans. Even the Port-O-San man cleaning up the "shitty mess" tells the camera that he has a son at Woodstock and another in Vietnam flying helicopters in the Demilitarized Zone. As Sheila Whiteley notes, the Vietnam War "is generally identified as the one great unifier of the counter-culture in that it demonstrated a concern for the developing world and, in particular, the racial and economic exploitation of other races" (Whiteley, 2004: 20). Indeed, just months before Woodstock, John Lennon and Yoko Ono staged their "bed-ins" for peace in Amsterdam and Montreal. The first actual performance we see (as opposed to hear) is by Richie Havens, who sings "Handsome Johnny," an anti-war song with verses that move from the Revolutionary War through the Korean War and depicts Johnny as the human sacrifice of all war. The character of "Johnny" evokes the World War I rallying cry of "Johnny get your gun," made popular in George M. Cohan's song "Over There," recorded by Al Jolson upon the United States' entry into the war, and later used by Dalton Trumbo as the title of his 1938 anti-war novel *Johnny Got His Gun*, which regained popularity during the Vietnam era.

Immediately after Havens sings the word "Korea," the film cuts to a shot of a helicopter flying past. It might be one of the helicopters that we later learn are shuttling musicians to and from the venue, but in this context it evokes an unmistakable link to Vietnam, as do the helicopters in Robert Altman's anti-war black comedy, *M*A*S*H* (1970), released the same year as *Woodstock*, although it is ostensibly set during the Korean conflict. Later, announcer Chip Monck comments that the US Army has deployed helicopters for medical help – "They're with us, they're not against us," Monck explains. The peace symbol on Alvin Lee's guitar is clearly visible during his long solo in Ten Years After's performance of "I'm Goin' Home," and Jefferson Airplane's performance of "Uncle Sam's Blues" (added in the Director's Cut) is explicitly anti-war in its lyrics: "I'm gonna do some fighting, of that I can be sure/And if I want to kill somebody, you know I won't have to break no kind of law." Joan Baez introduces the union organizing song "Joe Hill" by talking about her husband David, in jail for refusing the Draft (Plate 28), and Wadleigh also includes footage of Baez talking about David backstage before the song.

Country Joe McDonald's "I-Feel-Like-I'm-Fixin'-to-Die Rag," inspired by Kid Ory's old jazz standard "Muskrat Ramble," also protests the war in Vietnam, as well as middle-class conformity, with such lyrics as "Be the first one on your block/To have your boy come home in a box." McDonald wears an army shirt with sergeant's stripes, with flowing blue material sewn onto one sleeve – his apparel as well as his music an anti-war statement, like putting a flower in the gun barrel of a tank. His use of the first-person plural pronoun "we" in the rhetorical refrain "What are *we*

PLATE 28 *Woodstock*: Joan Baez performs the union protest song "Joe Hill."

fighting for?" suggests a situation mutually faced by all (McDonald himself in fact had already served a stint in the Navy). At one point in the song, Wadleigh cuts from McDonald performing to shots of people in the audience lip-syncing, which then seems to snowball into a mass sing-along, like a universal flash mob. The same idea informs a later montage of pot smokers accompanying Arlo Guthrie's performance of "Comin' into Los Angeles," a song about smuggling marijuana through customs. During the sequence, one toker even offers a hit to one of the cameramen, who takes it.

Humorously, Wadleigh prints the lyrics to Country Joe's song at the bottom of the image with a bouncing ball that hops from one word to the next as McDonald sings, in the manner of the popular sing-along gimmick that was often part of a movie theater's double-feature program during the classic studio era. The song thus becomes a communal sing-along both for the audience in the film and for the audience watching the film. The participatory nature of the moment is emphasized by Country Joe, who encourages the audience to sing more emphatically: "If you want to stop the war, you'll have to sing better than that." McDonald's solo performance at Woodstock actually happened at the beginning of the Festival, as he agreed to be pressed into service when several other scheduled groups were unable to arrive on time because of the swelling crowds, but Wadleigh places it toward the middle of the film to emphasize its thematic centrality (Bennett, 2004: 46).

The final musician we see in the film is legendary guitarist Jimi Hendrix, who plays three songs, the second of which is his now famous performance of "The Star-Spangled Banner." Significantly, at the beginning of the Director's Cut, the Warner Bros logo showing the obligatory rating ("R") for the film, which has been accompanied by part of this "solo," explodes in an animated graphic, making it seem, like Hendrix's performance, an assault on "the System." "The Star-Spangled Banner" was composed by Francis Scott Key after watching the British bombardment of Ft McHenry near Baltimore during the War of 1812, and Hendrix's treatment inevitably comments on its evocation of national identity and patriotic pride ("O say, can you see, by the dawn's early light/...That our flag was still there"). Hendrix deliberately situates his body and guitar in relation to the microphone to generate feedback as he plays. As one music critic has explained,

> The feedback and sustain provide a commentary on the flag itself as, at the words "broad stripes and bright stars," the sounds plummet and waiver. The attack, however, comes at the evocative "rocket's red glare" where Hendrix creates the sound of a fighter plane "coming out of a deep dive, the impact of bombs striking the earth and the cries of the Cambodian peasants." (Whiteley, 2004: 25, quoting Henderson)

Hendrix's aggressive aural treatment of the American national anthem subverts the patriotism intended in the original, more melodious composition, and has been regarded as nothing less than "an aural equivalent of burning the flag" (Moore, 2004: 78).

The solidarity of the Woodstock community is further demonstrated in the gathering storm which comes, significantly, just after Joe Cocker sings his version of the Lennon–McCartney tune "With a Little Help from My Friends." Dark, ominous clouds roll in and the wind is heard whipping on the sound track. Chip Monck suggests to the assembled multitude, "Hey, if you think really hard, maybe we can stop this rain," and the audience begins a chant of "no rain." The chant fails to stave off the Sunday afternoon storm, and a downpour ensues, but what is important is that the Woodstock community remains united in the face of the inclement weather. (One man even accuses "the fascist pigs" of seeding the clouds in order to disperse the crowd.) If the copious mud from the storm threatens to tarnish the dream, people steadfastly continue to be upbeat, turning the muddy hillsides into slides and generating spontaneous percussion and chanting, another suggestion of Woodstock as shared tribal ritual. As Mike Lang tells the camera, these people are communicating with each other.

Woodstock depicts the Woodstock community as vibrant and alive by conveying a sense of many things happening at once. Indeed, we don't actually see a musical performance (Richie Havens) until more than twenty minutes into the film. One way the film depicts the energy of the Woodstock Nation is by emphasizing the immense scale of the event, which it does throughout but particularly at the outset. *Woodstock* begins with an interview with a local merchant, Sidney Westerfield, who speaks directly to the camera, immediately extending the sense of the Woodstock community beyond the frame to include us as viewers. At one point, two men talk about how to control so many more people than had been expected; one of them compares this astonishing "influx of humanity" to the march of "man-eating" ants in South America. A local couple interviewed compare the size of the event to the annual Rose Bowl Parade in Pasadena, California. More than one local merchant speaks of the potential significant boost to the county's economy from the event, while sweeping helicopter shots take us across the concert site and the local environs to show us people as far as the eye can see. Jerry Garcia of The Grateful Dead tells the camera that it is "a biblical, epical, unbelievable scene." As he describes the flow of people, we see an aerial tracking shot of countless cars parked every which way like rows of toys. John Sebastian bluntly observes that the event is a "mindfucker of all time. I've never seen anything like this," while the farmer Max Yasgur is more circumspect in describing the Festival as the largest number of people ever assembled in one place.

The film periodically employs a split screen, occasionally even becoming a triptych, another way of suggesting the myriad things happening simultaneously at Woodstock and the impossibility of capturing an event of such epic magnitude within one frame or even one film. The first split screen occurs as Crosby, Stills and Nash begin "Wooden Ships." A long tracking shot on the right side past a procession of arriving cars stopped on the road is reminiscent of the famous, seemingly interminable traffic jam sequence shot in Jean-Luc Godard's *Weekend* (1967) (Plate 29). Shots of the moon and sun indicate that people are arriving throughout the night, without a let-up. We watch the super-trio perform the song at the same time as we also see construction continue on the mammoth stage: just as the audience is building, so the stage around which they will congregate is being built. The film first splits into three images when The Who perform "See Me, Feel Me" from their rock opera *Tommy*. The song's lyrics, repeated so plaintively by singer Roger Daltrey, sum up the film's

PLATE 29 *Woodstock*: The unexpected "influx of humanity" at the Festival becomes a utopian community.

communal vision through music: "See me, feel me, touch me, heal me/ Listening to you, I get the music." The three images, with the two at either end symmetrically reversed, emphasize The Who's renowned performative energy and Daltrey's fluid, flowing movements in his long-fringed vest. Reminiscent of a kaleidoscope, the triptych images also at once recall a tradition of European religious painting and invoke the psychedelic poster designs of Peter Max, a popular poster artist of the period.

When, in split screen, we see interviews with townspeople on the left and endless lines of newly arriving fans on the right, *Woodstock* demands in effect that we pay attention to two films simultaneously. And after Jefferson Airplane perform "Won't You Try," the split-screen montage of the "disaster area," with people lined up to use telephones and toilet facilities, essentially requires us to attend at once to two different sound tracks. As we become accustomed to these simultaneous images and sounds, they seem to conflate into one epic viewing experience – a spectator position that mirrors the multi-faceted but ultimately cohesive community represented within the film. This cohesion is expressed by the balance between images of the collective community and intimate shots of individuals. On the one hand, long shots from the stage show a sea of people stretching as far as the eye can see, while helicopter shots that sweep across the ground emphasize the enormity of the crowd. On the other hand, in big close-ups we see such details as the roof of Richie Havens' mouth or sweat dripping from his nose while he sings, and even the dust on John Sebastian's eyeglasses as he performs the gentle ballad "Younger Generation."

The periodic announcements over the sound system from Chip Monck on the stage further suggest this sense of community. His announcements are heard by all, sonically shared, like the music. These announcements include personal notes – "Marilyn Cohen, wherever you are, Greg wants you to meet him at the information booth 'cause he wants to marry you"; and "John Fogarty, return home immediately. Your father has been taken in for open heart surgery" – and helpful hints, such as the warning to stay away from the brown LSD, which "is not specifically too good." Monck's announcements make no moral judgments about the drug-taking, as he says them all in the same dry tone of voice: "If you feel like experimenting," he informs the audience regarding the brown acid, "only take half a tab. Thank you." At the end of the first night, he tells everyone, "Maybe the best thing for everybody to do unless you have a tent or someplace specific to go to – carve yourself out a piece of territory, say goodnight to your neighbour, and say thanks to yourself for making this the most peaceful, most pleasant day anybody's ever had in this kind of music."

As in other musicals, the music in *Woodstock* is not only about community, but also about sexuality, which is inextricably linked to the community theme. However, unlike so many fiction musicals, even those about rock 'n' roll as discussed in Chapter 3, the utopia of *Woodstock* celebrates sexual liberation rather than conformity. Cameras catch glimpses of couples disrobing to have sex in the bushes. The first Festival attendees interviewed, a young man named Jerry and the unnamed young woman with whom he is traveling, say they are not "going together" but living within a communal context; they reject the idea of a normative hetero-sexual relationship, and instead are part of "a family group" that is clearly different from the traditional nuclear family. "We ball and everything," she explains. But, she adds, there are no demands and both have their "freedom." She says they have come to the concert together, but they will not necessarily be there together. When asked by the cameraman about jealousy, both laugh and say possessiveness is not a factor. Their relation-ship, seemingly, is a perfect example of being "very free and easy," as Crosby, Stills and Nash sing in "Wooden Ships." As one of a group of young naked men in a stream says, "Everybody's happy, everybody's free."

Despite the utopia of Woodstock, at the same time, as Monck reminds everyone, this "doesn't mean that anything goes." The Woodstock Nation does not open the gates to anarchy, but rather, allows a path for spiritual exploration. As Festival co-producer Artie Kornfeld, seemingly ecstatic and holding a flower, explains after the decision to make it a free concert and take a loss on the venture, it has "nothing to do with money – nothing to do with tangible things." Richie Havens' rendition of "Motherless Child" contains a refrain in which he repeats the word "freedom" over and over, turning it into a chant. (Not coincidentally, it is just after his performance in the film that Lang and associates decide to make the concert free and an announcement is made that the welfare of everyone is more important than the potential profit.) Monck announces that forty-five doctors are on hand, "without pay, because they dig what this is into." The young man Jerry says that he, like everyone else, has come to Woodstock in search of enlightenment; as he says this, the montage on the left side of the split screen shows glimpses of various concertgoers and long shots of the vast crowd, applying his words to everyone there. The film cuts from here to Swami Satchidananda, an Indian yoga master, on the left side of the frame, the camera moving up his flowing grey beard as he speaks to the assembled multitude. America has helped the world materially, he says, but now the time has come for America to help the entire world spiritually as well. On the final day of the Festival, an announcer wakes everyone up, saying there are plans to feed 450,000 people breakfast in bed: "We're all feeding each other," he says; "We must be in heaven."

If *Woodstock* marked the heavenly heights of the counter-culture, The Rolling Stones' free concert at Altamont Speedway in northern California, which took place only four months later in December 1969, is commonly seen as signaling its end. Some of the bands who played at Altamont (Santana, Jefferson Airplane, and Crosby, Stills and Nash) also performed at Woodstock, and the concert was anticipated by many as the "West Coast Woodstock." The Stones were the final act, and during their performance of "Under My Thumb," which followed "Sympathy for the Devil," a member of the Hell's Angels motorcycle club, who were hired for concert security, stabbed a man in the audience to death. (The event was captured in Albert and David Maysles' documentary, *Gimme Shelter*, which was also released in 1970, several months after *Woodstock*.) The Angel was later acquitted of murder on the grounds of self-defense, as the fan had pulled a pistol from his jacket, but this was only the climax of the violence that characterized the Altamont concert.

Woodstock is fully aware that its utopian community was an ephemeral achievement, an ideal society impossible to maintain, as Wadleigh indicates in the film's ending. As Jimi Hendrix plays, appropriately, "Purple Haze," the last song performed in the film, we see shots of garbage and debris in the fields as the concert winds down and people begin to leave. A low-angle shot of a withered, miserable plant with one muddy leaf which has somehow survived the "influx of humanity" serves as a stark contrast to the lush shots of grass and flowers at the beginning. From today's vantage point, these images look almost post-apocalyptic. This sequence was added to the Director's Cut, perhaps as an afterthought about the ecological impact of the event from the perspective of hindsight. Then, after the closing credits, comes Crosby, Stills and Nash's "Find the Cost of Freedom," the film's last song on the sound track, which accompanies a necrology of prominent people from the "Woodstock Generation" who died before the release of the Director's Cut. Included are political figures such as John F. Kennedy, Malcolm X, Martin Luther King, Jr, all of whom died before the Festival itself, and some of the musicians who played at Woodstock (Paul Butterfield, Bob Hite, Keith Moon, Janis Joplin, Jimi Hendrix). The combination of politicians and social activists with musicians not only mourns the passing of a generation, but also indicates the political and social power of popular music, fully realized in the transient moment known as Woodstock.

CHAPTER 8

PHANTOM OF THE PARADISE (1974)

Phantom of the Paradise is a musical horror comedy, a darkly funny backstage musical about a devilish rock impresario, Swan (Paul Williams), and his attempt to steal the music of a gifted musician, Winslow Leach (Bill Finley). At first a box-office and critical failure, the film has since acquired a cult following. There have been a few other horror musical hybrids, including *Nudist Colony of the Dead* (1991), *The Happiness of the Katakuris* (1981), Michael Jackson's influential music video *Thriller* (1983), *Corpse Bride* (2005), *Sweeney Todd* (2007), and, of course, the earlier cult phenomenon *The Rocky Horror Picture Show* (1975). But while these other films also employ popular music, often for satiric effect, *Phantom of the Paradise* is the only one whose satiric target is precisely the institution of popular music itself. The film's production numbers mock the entire history of rock music as little more than changing generic fashion, dictated by the whims of a few taste makers.

The film was written and directed by Brian De Palma, an important member of the New Hollywood generation of directors who emerged in the 1970s after the decline of the studio system. Many of these directors, including Steven Spielberg, George Lucas, William Friedkin, Peter Bogdanovich, Francis Ford Coppola, and Martin Scorsese, were collectively known as the "movie brats" because most had studied film in university and were knowledgeable about film history and theory. They began their careers at the same time that the studio system was crumbling

The Hollywood Film Musical, First Edition. Barry Keith Grant.

and the auteur theory had gained popular currency, thus allowing them considerable opportunity for artistic freedom. Consequently, these directors often made revisionist genre movies that consciously reworked classic traditions. Friedkin's *The French Connection* (1971), Scorsese's *Mean Streets* (1973), and Coppola's *The Godfather* (1972) all took the crime film in new directions, as did De Palma with the remake of *Scarface* (1983), *Carlito's Way* (1993), both with Al Pacino, and *The Untouchables* (1987). But before De Palma's exploration of the gangster film, his early work was often in horror, and he first attracted wide attention with his stylish contribution to the genre in *Sisters* (1973).

One distinctive aspect of De Palma's cine-literacy is his penchant for quotations from and homages to other films and directors. *Blow Out* (1981) borrows considerably from Michelangelo Antonioni's *Blow-Up* (1966) and Coppola's *The Conversation* (1974), and the climactic shootout in the train station in *The Untouchables* references the Odessa Steps sequence from Sergei Eisenstein's *Battleship Potemkin* (1925), one of the most famous sequences in film history, with its baby carriage bouncing down the steps in the middle of a crossfire. While some have regarded De Palma as "the most idiosyncratic major director at work in American movies today" (Rose, 1982: 88), others have considered his work largely derivative, particularly in its referencing of the films of the "master of suspense," Alfred Hitchcock. Hitchcockian references appear throughout De Palma's work: the derailing amusement park ride in *The Fury* (1978) recalls the careening carousel in the climax of Hitchcock's *Strangers on a Train* (1951); *Dressed to Kill* (1980) takes its premise of a schizophrenic murderer from *Psycho* (1960); *Body Double* (1984) borrows the plot of Hitchcock's *Rear Window* (1954); and *Obsession* (1976) is based on *Vertigo* (1958). But, as this discussion of *Phantom of the Paradise* suggests, De Palma's references, including those to Hitchcock, in fact resonate with thematic meaning.

Phantom of the Paradise contains elements of many horror films and stories, including *Psycho*. The story is a loosely adapted mixture of *The Phantom of the Opera*, originally a serialized novel by Gaston Leroux published in 1909–10, adapted to film several times and also later as a musical by Andrew Lloyd Webber; Oscar Wilde's novel *The Picture of Dorian Gray* (1890); and the story of Faust, a figure of German legend, and the subject both of plays by Marlowe and Goethe and of F.W. Murnau's 1923 film. The Faust legend, about a scholar who makes a deal with the devil for unlimited knowledge in return for his soul, is a particularly appropriate one to adapt to the world of popular music, for not only is there an identifiable genre of soul music, but the term "soul" in music culture generally refers to one's ability to translate true emotion into music, to be, in short, a true musical artist. Among *Phantom of the Paradise*'s numerous other references are homages to such additional classic horror movies as *The Cabinet of Dr Caligari* (1920), one of the earlier masterpieces of German Expressionist cinema, and James Whale's 1931 version of *Frankenstein* with Boris Karloff. Indeed, like Frankenstein's monster, *Phantom of the Paradise* is a patchwork creation, a text stitched together from multiple pop culture references. However, this is not to say that *Phantom of the Paradise* is derivative or unoriginal; rather, as we shall see, its dense network of allusions are thematically central to its critique of popular music and, by extension, popular culture generally.

The importance of the film's references is signaled from the very beginning, even before the credits. A voice-over narration, spoken (uncredited) by Rod Serling, accompanies a spiraling image of a dead bird, the logo for Death Records in the film's story, providing the back story about Swan, the record company's mysterious owner, and his rise to fame. Serling had been the host and primary writer of the popular television show *The Twilight Zone*, which aired on CBS from 1959 through 1964, and which featured stories with science fiction, fantasy, and horror premises. The show was so popular that, along with its host, it became inextricably associated with the strange, the supernatural, and the suspenseful. In addition, the spiraling image of death suggests a spinning vortex, what Edgar Allan Poe called the horrifying "descent into the maelstrom." The image of the dead bird, which is also the very last image of the film, is the first of several references to *Psycho*: when motel proprietor Norman Bates (Anthony Perkins) enters the room where the film's protagonist, the aptly named Marion *Crane* (Janet Leigh), has just been murdered, he knocks a framed picture of a bird off the wall as he recoils in horror.

Serling explains that although his past is a mystery, Swan was responsible for exporting the blues to Britain, for bringing the British Invasion to America, and even for creating the hybrid genre of folk-rock. Now he is looking for a new sound. A fade-in after the credits shows why: the vocal group The Juicy Fruits, whom Serling has told us were single-handedly responsible for the "nostalgia wave of the 1970s," are onstage singing the film's opening number, "Goodbye, Eddie, Goodbye." Clearly, their sound is old-fashioned and the time is right for Swan to create another new style. The Juicy Fruits' performance style parodies doo-wop, one of the earliest rock vocal styles, even as their name connotes the scorned genre of Bubble-Gum, catchy pop melodies and arrangements aimed at pre-teen consumers. The group's ironic performance and exaggeration of the doo-wop style specifically recall the rock group Sha Na Na, who were popular at the time. Sha Na Na dressed in gold lamé leather suits, sported retro pompadours, and sang classic '50s rock 'n' roll in a campy style. The group achieved national fame after performing at Woodstock in 1969, preceding Jimi Hendrix and appearing for all of a minute and a half in Michael Wadleigh's 1970 rockumentary of the Festival, discussed in the previous chapter. Subsequently they had a very popular hit television show, *Sha Na Na*, from 1977 to 1982. In *Phantom of the Paradise*, The Juicy Fruits' harmonies recall The Diamonds' 1957 hit song "Little Darlin'," which was one of the tunes sung by Sha Na Na at Woodstock.

"Goodbye, Eddie, Goodbye" evokes the rock subgenre of the tragic romance, songs like "Tell Laura I Love Her" and "Last Kiss," both about lovers dying in car crashes. The lyrics in this case tell the "tragic story" of Eddie and his sister, Mary Louise, who needs money for a live-saving operation. Eddie thus decides to become an "overnight sensation" and then commit suicide because the public has a morbid fascination for "post-mortem stars." In the climax of the song the lead singer stabs himself with a stage knife and falls twitching to the ground as he croons about "the sacrifice you made, we can't believe the price you paid for love." The maudlin story of the song foreshadows the unfortunate fate that will befall Winslow, aka the Phantom, who dies because of his devotion to his music and to the female singer, Phoenix, his muse.

After the song, Arnold Philbin (George Memmoli), Swan's right-hand man, complains to Swan about Annette, a female singer he claims he took out of the Church and groomed for stardom but who has rejected him by deciding to manage her own career and doing benefit concerts for "starving gook orphans." Philbin speaks directly to the camera, and although we have yet to see Swan, we get a sense of his power in the music industry when he agrees to destroy her career for the angry Philbin, dismissing the favor as no big deal: "Is that all?... Annette is finished. She's through. Washed up." Philbin protests that Annette is at the top of the charts, although Swan shrugs off his concern by observing that this may be true today but that by tomorrow she'll be forgotten. In this scene, crucially, Philbin's direct address to the camera immediately places the audience in Swan's position, suggesting the symbiotic relationship of producer and consumer, the fact that Swan's power is dependent upon the acceptance of fans.

As Philbin talks to the camera in the balcony in the left foreground of the image, we see someone in the background setting up at the piano on the stage and begin playing. Swan is impressed by what he hears, and as he interrupts Philbin to listen, De Palma cuts to a close-up of Winslow, the camera then sweeping around him in a circular motion as he sings, in a parody of the cliché of visual romanticism found, for example, at the end of Claude Lelouch's romantic hit *A Man and a Woman* (1966). De Palma later used this same circling camera movement at the end of *Obsession* in the delirious romantic fantasy of Elizabeth (Genevieve Bujold) as she meets her duplicitous husband, Michael (Cliff Robertson). Here, it similarly suggests the musician's intense absorption in his creative energy, his artistic vision oblivious to such mundane worldly considerations as money. But, as we shall see, it is just this naïve narcissism that makes him vulnerable to the strategies of Swan in the first place. In his song, "Faust," Winslow sings, "As I lived my role/I swore I'd sell my soul/for one love," the lyrics again foreshadowing the poor singer's impending fate.

An abrupt cut to a pair of white-gloved hands in the balcony box slowly offering a series of hand claps is our first glimpse of Swan. The shot is yet another of De Palma's references, recalling in its composition the ego-maniacal protagonist of Orson Welles' *Citizen Kane* (1941), who insists on clapping after the horrible opera debut of his talentless wife Susan Alexander. Just as the rest of the audience in *Citizen Kane* politely follow suit and applaud after Kane, intimidated by his power and wealth, so Swan controls the public's taste. The ironic casting of the diminutive Paul Williams, composer of the lyrics for such gold records as The Carpenters' "We've Only Just Begun" and "Rainy Days and Mondays," as a towering figure in the music industry suggests more than a passing resemblance to Phil Spector, the Svengali-like producer who created the "wall of sound" style of such girl groups as The Ronettes and The Crystals, and who worked with many other recording artists, including The Righteous Brothers, Leonard Cohen, and The Beatles. As Michael Bliss describes Williams, "His baby blonde hair and pudgy, virtually infantile features suggest a well-fed homunculus or an other-worldly changeling left on someone's doorstep" (Bliss, 1983: 32) – in other words, an ideal choice for the role of the strange Swan.

Swan decides that Winslow's music, but not "that creep" Winslow himself, would be perfect for the big opening of his new rock palace, the Paradise. The mise-en-scène here, with Winslow shown very small in the far background, suggests the power dynamic between the characters and how Winslow will soon be at the mercy of Swan's nefarious plans. Philbin visits Winslow, telling him how much Swan loved his music. Delighted, Winslow notes, "If Mr Swan would produce my music, the whole world would listen to me." Still, he cannot give Philbin "two or three up numbers" because he has written a rock cantata, an ambitious extended musical work that tells, appropriately, the story of Faust. The philistine

Philbin, not getting the reference, asks, "Faust? What label's he on?" Winslow becomes violently angry, revealing his own monstrously repressed inner nature, slamming Philbin against the wall as he insists, "I'm not going to let my music be mutilated by those greaseballs." Instead, he gives him the entire work-in-progress when Philbin promises that Swan will produce Winslow's first album.

One month later, having heard nothing, Winslow comes to the offices of Death Records. The receptionist checks her files, and finds his name among such others as Bette Midler, Alice Cooper, Dick Clark, and Kris Kristofferson – a joke about other minimal musical talents who perhaps have made it big in the pop music industry by selling their souls or, alternatively, because they have none. Unfortunately, next to Winslow's name is printed the instruction "Never to be seen," and Winslow is promptly and unceremoniously tossed out of the building by Swan's bouncers. Their denim jackets suggest motorcycle gangs like the appositely named Hell's Angels, who served as "security" at The Rolling Stones' infamous Altamont concert captured in the rockumentary *Gimme Shelter* (1970), discussed in the previous chapter. Winslow follows Swan to his palatial estate, the Swanage, and as he walks toward it we hear him on the sound track singing, "I never thought I'd get to meet the Devil/Never thought I'd see him face to face." Stepping inside, he starts to cross a black-and-white tiled floor, suggesting his status as pawn in Swan's game, when he hears a great caterwauling of women's voices – one with a heavy New York accent that sounds as bad as, if not worse than, the greaseball Juicy Fruits – rehearsing his cantata. His attention is drawn to one of them, Phoenix (Jessica Harper) – also the name of the Arizona city where Marion Crane lives in *Psycho* – an aspiring singer whom Winslow thinks has the ability to do his music justice, and the two are immediately attracted to each other in the typical manner of romance and musical films (Plate 30).

In this case, though, the magical connection is short-lived, as the women are ushered into their auditions by Swan's minions. Along with Winslow, who is refused entry, through the closing doors we glimpse one of these "auditions," which is nothing more than an orgy on a casting couch. Phoenix, an aspiring artist with integrity, is also tossed out when she refuses to participate. After Winslow tries unsuccessfully to sneak back inside dressed in drag, he is framed by corrupt policemen for possession of drugs and handed a life sentence in – ironically – Sing-Sing Prison, where he is "volunteered" to participate in the Dental Health Research Program funded by the Swan Foundation. This sequence is conveyed in a rapid montage emulating Warner Bros crime movies from the classic studio era. One of this movies is references in the next shot, where Winslow, now

PLATE 30 *Phantom of the Paradise*: Winslow Leach (William Finley) rehearses his music with the aspiring singer Phoenix (Jessica Harper) (Brian De Palma, 1974; Producer: Edward R. Pressman).

working in the prison rehab center, his teeth replaced with metal dentures, hears an announcement for The Juicy Fruits' hit recording of his music and he freaks out, attacking a guard in a long shot that recalls the psychotic criminal Cody Jarrett (James Cagney) doing the same thing in the prison mess hall in *White Heat* (1949). If Jarrett has been driven mad by his overbearing mother, Winslow is similarly pushed over the edge of sanity by the monstrous manipulations of someone he had trusted.

The involuntary extraction of Winslow's teeth and their prosthetic replacement visually suggests the way the musical artist's "voice," her or his distinctive personal vision and style, is often at the mercy of producers and commercial considerations. This reading is reinforced shortly after when Winslow's head is caught in the record press at the Death Records factory and his face disfigured like his namesake, the Phantom of the Opera. The idea of the mediated manipulation of the artist has its most eloquent statement, though, in the later stunning, slow tracking shot, when Winslow is completing his music for Swan, as the camera glides slowly along the various cables in the studio leading from Winslow to the control room while his voice gradually changes from a harsh croak to a smooth croon on the sound track (Plate 31). By the end of the shot, Winslow's voice has changed completely, restored to its original pleasant tone.

Escaping prison, Winslow returns to the city and breaks into the company headquarters of Death Records, where he begins destroying the stock of The Juicy Fruits' *Faust*. After he is caught in the record press and his face is smashed, he enters the record company's wardrobe department and finds the outfit and silver helmet that will transform him into the eponymous Phantom. A swirling newspaper headline informs us that the Paradise is about to open and, in *Variety* jargon, that "Fruits Preem Swan's Faust," while a small item beneath it dismisses Winslow's fate with "Mad Tunesmith Bites Bullet." The relative size of the two news items indicates the extent of media manipulation also at work in the music industry, for, as Charles Foster Kane says in *Citizen Kane*, "If the headline is big enough, it makes the news big enough."

The Juicy Fruits, now renamed The Beach Bums, rehearse Winslow's music, suddenly transformed into pop surfer music harmonies reminiscent of The Beach Boys, as a split screen shows us the Phantom setting and planting a bomb in a prop automobile. The stage is decorated with go-go girls in bikinis and two-dimensional ocean waves, the flatness of the props (but not the girls!) a comment on the aesthetic depth of the music.

PLATE 31 *Phantom of the Paradise*: Winslow as the Phantom in the recording studio with the devilish producer Swan (Paul Williams).

The former greaseballs, now wearing blonde wigs, sing "Upholstery," wailing in Beach Boy harmonies that "Carburetors, man, that's what life is all about" and praising the "Upholstery, where my baby sits up close to me." Now, what had begun as a serious work about love and the soul has been reduced to adolescent concerns about cars and girls – a perfect example of the cultural process that Thomas Doherty has called the "juvenilization" of American culture (Doherty, 1988). The timer on the bomb ticks away throughout the scene, as in the famous opening of Welles' *Touch of Evil* (1958), where an explosive device is also set in the trunk of a car. In *Phantom*, one of The Beach Bums protests to Philbin that he has to leave because he hears something like a bomb ticking in his head, just as the woman passenger in the car says to the border guard in Welles' film. Then, as in *Touch of Evil*, the car explodes.

Glimpsing the Phantom, Swan realizes what is happening, and when the Phantom threateningly confronts him, Swan calmly greets him and disarms him by promising Winslow the chance to have his music produced the way he wants. "Trust me," Swan urges insincerely, as he steps into a close-up accompanied by ominous organ notes on the sound track. Evidently, Winslow does, as the next scene shows Swan holding auditions where Winslow chooses Phoenix when she sings "Special to Me" as her audition piece. The song, written by Paul Williams, who plays Swan, is addressed to her romantic partner, whose ambitions have made him work too hard to become "somebody special," even though he will always be special to her. She condemns "all evil that takes possession/Until your pipe dreams become obsessions" and speculates that he must under "some kind of spell." Unknowingly, she not only sings about Winslow's unbounded artistic ambition, but also what will become of her own situation later after Swan seduces her and gets her to sign one of his devilish contracts. As she sings, she swirls around on the stage, the circular movements of her dance expressing her self-absorbed nature, like Winslow's.

When next we see Winslow, he is in a studio within the bowels of the Paradise, wearing an electronic box on his chest over his Phantom costume and playing and rasping his music as the camera tracks to Swan in the control room (one of the actual recording studios of The Record Plant, one of the most important American studios, where, among others, Jimi Hendrix, Bruce Springsteen, Lady Gaga, and Kiss have cut albums). Winslow's voice – dubbed here, and elsewhere, by Williams, adding an extra layer of irony – is modulated at the complex console by Swan ("Filters! Dolbys!"), who then abruptly unplugs Winslow's box, foreshadowing his secret intentions and demonstrating his power not only to shape Winslow's voice but also to silence it. Then, out of nowhere, Swan produces a massive contract, and even though it contains such absurd clauses as "All articles that are excluded shall be deemed included," Winslow, inspired by his artistic vision, signs in blood. To a montage of the Phantom feverishly working around the clock to complete his cantata, we hear him (actually Williams) perform the ballad "The Phantom's Theme (Beauty and the Beast)." In the lyrics he acknowledges his own collusion in his artistic destruction ("To work it out I let them in/ All the good guys and the bad guys that I've been") and anticipates his sacrifice in the climactic concert ("Like a circus on parade... I wander through an angry crowd and wonder what became of me").

Meanwhile, Swan demotes Phoenix to one of the background singers and auditions possible replacements as he sets about to sabotage Winslow's art. A montage of auditions shows him considering performers of different musical styles, including a country singer with a guitar, a female soul trio, and a screeching glam rock performer, Beef (Gerritt Graham), whom Swan chooses because he is clearly the least talented and the most inappropriate. As he explains to Philbin, "No one listens to lyrics anyway." Beef is a neurotic, whining prima donna who clearly will destroy Winslow's music. Later, in rehearsal, he throws his guitar down and pouts, "Man, you better get yourself a castrato for this, it's a little out of my range." Reaching a high note, he falls over in his elevator shoes reminiscent of those worn by Boris Karloff as the creature in *Frankenstein*, and comically struggles to stand upright again.

At an airport press conference, Swan introduces his new star to the waiting world. Swan is dressed in a black cape and top hat that recall Werner Krause's costume as the controlling tyrant in *The Cabinet of Dr Caligari*, while Beef appears out of a coffin, like the somnambulist Cesare, Caligari's puppet. The reference here is particularly appropriate because the devilish producer Swan is a Svengali figure who hypnotizes the masses to accept whatever product he decides to promote, as we already have seen in his pronouncements regarding the fate of Annette and will soon see again in the unthinking response of the audience to Beef's death onstage during the Paradise's opening night performance. Announcing his new discovery at the press conference, Swan unintentionally foreshadows Beef's fate in saying that his performance will be "live – on the Death label."

The little room where Winslow completes his cantata suggests the labels, the little boxes, into which producers try to make performers comfortably fit, as in the recognizable genre types that Swan has just auditioned. When Winslow finishes *Faust*, Swan has him sealed in, but Winslow manages to escape when he realizes what is going on. Primping in front of the mirror with curlers in his hair and deer antlers protruding from his belt, Beef hears the Phantom's piercing cry of anguish at being duped again by Swan and, freaked out, he tells Philbin that the Paradise is haunted. As Beef showers before the big opening, De Palma gives us the film's funniest reference: he repeats Hitchcock's shot when Marion Crane takes her infamous shower in the Bates Motel in *Psycho* and Norman enters the bathroom. Here, we see the Phantom wielding a knife beyond the shower curtain, just as in *Psycho* we see Norman about to attack an unaware Marion – but then, instead of stabbing him with the knife after he uses it to rip open the shower curtain, the Phantom unexpectedly sticks a toilet plunger in Beef's face.

Warning him never to sing his music again, that it is only for Phoenix, the Phantom says, "Anyone else who tries it, dies," as he removes the plunger from Beef's startled face with a sickening slurp and the shocked singer slides down the tiled shower wall like the dying Marion. In panic, Beef wants to flee home to his mother in Cincinatti. Philbin tries to calm Beef down by suggesting that he has been hallucinating from taking drugs, to which Beef indignantly replies, "I know drug-real from real-real." Yet although he complains that "the karma is so thick around here you need an aqualung to breathe," Beef is coerced into going on with the show – a decision that in musicals is normally triumphant, but in *Phantom of the Paradise* is clearly unwise.

For music critic Arnold Shaw, glitter rock, named after British singer Gary Glitter, features "odd and outrageous costumes, makeup, hairdos, props, and antics . . . in an effort to add a visual dimension to a musical program. When the artist goes beyond visual appeal into the viscera, and, through the use of violence and sex, goes beyond mere entertainment and amusement, we have Shock Rock" (Shaw, 1982: 141). And this is exactly what we have in the climactic opening night performance at the Paradise. The curtain opens to reveal a set that could have come from *Caligari*, with stage lights flashing like lightning. The Juicy Fruits, now renamed The Undeads, are dressed in costumes that resemble a cross between *Caligari*'s Cesare and Kiss. The Undeads play electric guitars with necks that look like scythes or swords (playing on the colloquial term "axe" for this instrument), swinging them as if they are slicing the fans in the audience, who cheer everything indiscriminately. The death metal style of The Undeads seems to become literal as one guitar neck slices off the prop hand of a fan. For a moment we might wonder whether this is part of the show or an actual attack, part of the film's horror elements, thus putting us briefly in the same unaware position as the spectators at the show. Other body parts are collected from the audience as The Undeads sing "Somebody Super Like You," about creating a perfect man, complete with a

"Hollywood smile and a perfect profile" to which the masses would pledge devotion. The collected body parts are given to nurses on the stage, who pretend to stitch them together, and in a stylized variation of the creation scene in Whale's *Frankenstein*, the creature is hoisted to the roof in a box to collect life-giving electricity from the lightning.

When the box is lowered, Beef awakens as a glitter Frankenstein monster and prances around the stage singing "Life at Last" with a delirious combination of macho and effeminate gestures. He plays his guitar with his teeth like Jimi Hendrix and struts with it at his pelvis like a phallic extension, a hilarious parody of heavy metal performance style that mocks the very notion of what Simon Frith and Angela McRobbie four years later would refer to as "cockrock": "music in which performance is an explicit, crude, and often aggressive expression of male sexuality." As they describe the style, "mikes and guitars are phallic symbols; the music is loud, rhythmically insistent, built around techniques of arousal and climax; the lyrics are assertive and arrogant, though the exact words are less significant than the vocal styles involved, the shouting and the screaming" (Frith and McRobbie, 1990: 374). Speaking of phallic symbols – like an outraged Zeus, the Phantom, hidden in the rafters, sends a neon lightning bolt at the stage, barbecuing Beef. The audience, indifferent to all but the show, regards his electrocution as part of the spectacle and continues cheering wildly, even as Philbin douses the smoldering flame that once was Beef with a fire extinguisher. "Look at them – they're really entertained. They never want the show to stop," says Swan. Phoenix comes onstage at Philbin's order to fill in for Beef, rising, as her name suggests, as if from his ashes. While the Phantom follows her with a spotlight from above, she sings "Old Souls," an inoffensive, sentimental ballad about the power of love which, in the context of her immanent sellout, can only seem hollow.

Just as in *42nd Street* (1933) Peggy (Ruby Keeler) goes on stage as a nobody understudy and comes back a star, Phoenix suddenly finds herself famous (Plate 32). But Swan quickly seduces her with drugs and the promise of fame. "I'll give them whatever they want," she says passively, now having sold her soul, the very thing she had decried in "Special to Me" earlier. The feathered wrap she wears at this point suggests that she has become another "dead bird," like the Death Records logo. The Phantom whisks her away from her frenzied fans and takes her to the roof, where he reveals his true identity to Phoenix and tries to warn her about Swan, but she refuses to believe him and recoils in horror when he unmasks himself à la the Phantom of the Opera. Back at the Swanage, the Phantom observes Swan and Phoenix through the skylight making love,

PLATE 32 *Phantom of the Paradise:* Phoenix seizes the opportunity to become a star at Swan's rock palace, the Paradise.

the rain streaming down the window through which we see him, making it seem as if tears are streaking his face. His grotesque appearance keeps him forever excluded from such intimacy, like Frankenstein's creature.

And also like that poor creature, the Phantom chooses a wedding day for his vengeance. A headline in *Rolling Stone* magazine announces that Swan and Phoenix plan to marry onstage during the finale of *Faust* the next evening. The Phantom learns that the producer made a pact with the devil twenty years ago – that is, dating from the time of *Phantom of the Paradise*'s release, the mid-1950s, the time of the birth of rock 'n' roll – as he was about a to commit suicide because he was getting old. Swan agreed to the standard deal with the devil, dismissing the importance of his soul, unintentionally commenting not only on his fate in the film's narrative but also on the middle-of-the-road pop style of the performer playing him. The Phantom realizes that Swan is planning to have Phoenix killed live on television ("That's entertainment," as Swan observes), turning it into a literal shotgun wedding with a hired assassin. In homage to the suspenseful climax of the Cold War thriller *The Manchurian Candidate* (1962), another film about brainwashing, he rushes to the rescue, knocking aside the shooter's rifle at the last moment so that Philbin, officiating at the ceremony dressed as a bishop, is shot instead. The Phantom swings across the stage like Errol Flynn, ripping the mask off Swan's face, revealing a hideous decomposing visage brought about by Winslow's earlier destruction of Swan's videotaped contracts. But the show, with everyone dancing, never stops, and the crowd is whipped into a frenzy by the onstage spectacle. Swan's body is borne aloft by the hysterical crowd as he dies. Winslow, also dying, removes his mask to reveal his own disfigured face, and, cheered on by the crowd, crawls on the floor toward the shocked Phoenix, accompanied by members of the audience pleased to be involved in the performance. As Winslow collapses, Phoenix finally recognizes him.

In the penultimate shot before the closing credits, the camera pulls back in an overhead view that shows all the audience writhing in rhythm, but there is no discernible pattern, no harmony, in their movements as in a Busby Berkeley shot. Indeed, the image looks more like the famous overhead reverse zoom of the insane asylum as hell in *The Snake Pit* (1948). The ironic association of the Paradise with hell is reinforced throughout the film by the periodic shots of Swan's henchmen, dressed like Hell's Angels.

While *Phantom of the Paradise* is part of a cycle of rock movies that concentrated capitalist exploitation and greed into the single character of the producer, who comes to represent the entire music industry, it stands apart from the rest. In *Good Times* (1967), the greedy producer Mordicus (George Sanders) tries to convince innocents Sonny and Cher to sacrifice their "I Got You, Babe" solidarity for a more commercial style; and in *The Rose* (1979), a high–powered manager (Alan Bates) pushes his singer (Bette Midler) to the point of suicide. In screenwriter/star Paul Simon's *One-Trick Pony* (1980), the rock artist is forced either to repeat his past without conviction, as empty nostalgia like The Juicy Fruits, or to accept the gimmicky production values from his insensitive producer (Lou Reed). These movies employ what Roland Barthes refers to as "Operation Margarine," an ideological strategy that "immunizes the contents of the collective imagination by means of a small inoculation of acknowledged evil; one thus protects it against the risk of a generalized subversion" (Barthes, 1972: 150). Any real social critique in these musicals is ultimately recuperable by the genre's mythic values of community and entertainment, as the goodness of the system survives the excessive greed and power of the few individuals who, it is implied, are just the rotten apples in an otherwise fresh barrel. *Phantom of the Paradise*, by contrast, takes as its target the industry at large, which includes its audience. A dissolve from the overhead shot of the frenzied crowd to the final shot of the Death Records logo makes it look for a moment as if the audience is hellishly writhing within the body of the dead bird, thus ending the film with a final condemnation of the audience's collusion in its own manipulation. As Beef had sung in "Life at Last," "Do you realize that all of you donated something horrible you hated that is part of you/I'm your nightmares comin' true/I am your crime."

It would not be stretching too much to read *Phantom of the Paradise* biographically, seeing Winslow as a self-portrait of the artist as victim. Winslow is a well-intentioned but naïve visionary destroyed by the industry, just as the idiosyncratic Young Turk director Brian De Palma ran afoul of Hollywood with *Get to Know Your Rabbit* (1972), his first Hollywood project and a film that was taken away from him and re-edited by Warner Bros. But clearly the film's satiric sights are set much wider. As De Palma has said, the film is "about this whole culture. That it is obsessed with death, with destroying yourself, burning yourself up, consuming yourself for entertainment and amusement . . . a culture looking for bigger and better highs . . . . It is a very de-sensitized, de-emotionalized culture" (Bartholomew, 1975: 10). That's entertainment, indeed.

CHAPTER 9

PENNIES FROM HEAVEN (1981) AND *ACROSS THE UNIVERSE* (2007)

Both *Pennies from Heaven* and *Across the Universe* are set in the past, in different decades of the previous century – the 1930s and 1960s, respectively. The two films are similar stylistically to some extent, as both rely heavily on postmodern strategies of pastiche and intertextuality to construct their historical vision. Importantly, though, their take on these two decades is radically different: *Pennies from Heaven* views Depression-era Chicago as a predatory world where only the cynical survive and naïve romantics are doomed, whereas *Across the Universe* instead embraces love as a panacea for more worldly problems. Yet despite their profound ideological differences, the two films share a view of popular music as a crucial element of social history, even as the key to the period's distinctive cultural mindset.

Pennies from Heaven was based on a 1978 BBC television series written by British writer Dennis Potter, who wrote mostly for television but also for film, and adapted by him to the American setting of Chicago during the Great Depression. Like his best-known work, the series *The Singing Detective* (1986), *Pennies from Heaven* freely mixes fantasy and reality largely through the use of popular music as a shaping influence on his characters' imaginations. The film was choreographed by Danny Daniels, a veteran of stage and film, and directed by Herbert Ross, who also directed the musical version of *Goodbye, Mr Chips* (1969), *Funny Lady*

The Hollywood Film Musical, First Edition. Barry Keith Grant.
© 2012 Barry Keith Grant. Published 2012 by Blackwell Publishing Ltd.

(1975) with Barbra Streisand, the astonishingly successful *Footloose* (1984), and two dramatic films about classical dance, *The Turning Point* (1977), with Anne Bancroft and Shirley MacLaine, and *Dancers* (1987), with Mikhail Baryshnikov. *Pennies from Heaven* was nominated for three Academy Awards – Best Costume Design, Best Sound, and Best Writing, Screenplay Based on Material from Another Medium – but did not win any. Potter himself lost in the Best Adapted Screenplay category to *On Golden Pond* (1981), a popular sentimental drama featuring classical-era Hollywood stalwarts Henry Fonda and Katharine Hepburn. Neither did *Pennies from Heaven* do well at the box office, grossing less than $10 million on its release against a budget of $22 million.

One reason for the film's commercial failure was the confusion of audiences in seeing Steve Martin in a serious role after establishing a comic persona with his many appearances on television's long-running comedy show *Saturday Night Live*. *Pennies from Heaven* was Martin's second starring vehicle after the hit comedy *The Jerk* (1979) and his first dramatic role. And while there is some humor in the surprising and unconventional musical numbers in *Pennies from Heaven*, Martin's conflicted sheet-music salesman, Arthur Parker, is as much tragic as he is comic. Most of Martin's subsequent roles have been in comedies as well, although his character in David Mamet's thriller *The Spanish Prisoner* (1997) also was enriched by the ambiguity of his established comic persona, as it is in *Pennies from Heaven*.

If earlier Hollywood musicals seek to integrate story and production numbers into an illusion of a unified, utopian world, *Pennies from Heaven* emphasizes the gap between music and its production to deconstruct that illusion. Most obviously, the voices are only lip-synced, and they are not the voices of the actors on screen. Ironically, this gives *Pennies from Heaven* a greater truth than many more conventional musicals, including *Singin' in the Rain* (1952) and *West Side Story* (1961), in which the characters lip-sync their voices – or someone else's – with the sound recorded at another time and mixed in on the final sound track later. In *Pennies from Heaven*, by contrast, the production numbers – all based on hit recordings of the 1930s by such artists as Rudy Vallee, Connie Boswell, and Bing Crosby (who not coincidentally starred in the 1936 musical comedy *Pennies from Heaven*) – are contextualized as the fantasies and the inner desires of the characters. The disjunction between the person in the image and the sound of the person on the sound track shatters the illusion of the classical musical's utopian plentitude since it is clear to viewers that the characters in the film are not actually singing, or pretending to be actually singing, the music that we are hearing. This is true of all the musical numbers, but especially in scenes such as when Martin lip-syncs to the female voice of Connie Boswell in "It's the Girl" or to the voice of Bing, a singer whose voice was so distinctive that, according to Leslie Gourse, "almost any American can recognize [it] . . . with lightning speed" (Gourse, 1984: 21).

The film's narrative further emphasizes the disparity between the sunny myths of pop music and the harsh realities of the film's unpleasant world, which is depicted more like film noir from the next decade than the 1930s musicals of either Busby Berkeley or Fred Astaire and Ginger Rogers. At the nadir of Arthur's relationship with Eileen (Bernadette Peters), for example, the couple are in a seedy hotel room, Arthur wearing a T-shirt like Burt Lancaster in *The Killers* (1946) and *I Walk Alone* (1948); the hotel's neon marquee outside blinks on and off, evoking one of the most familiar visual conventions of noir imagery. This noirish mise-en-scène stands in stark opposition to Arthur's brightly lit musical fantasies like "Yes, Yes," the opulent lighting here paralleling the optimism of the number. The film's initial images behind the opening credits are significant. First, we see a sky with beautifully burnished clouds, behind which the sun is about to peep (or is it, instead, being obscured?), its rays beaming promisingly in golden shafts, evoking the heaven in the title. But then the camera descends through a layer of ominously black clouds and a thunderstorm with rain and lightning to a dark and damp Chicago street. As the credits end, there is a cut to a close-up of Arthur waking up in the morning, as if we are coming down from the heights of his dreams to the prosaic realities of his real life. This opening encapsulates the film's trajectory of undermining the typically upbeat ideology of the classic musical by emphasizing its values as idealistic, false, and even dangerous.

In the plot, Arthur is a traveling sheet-music salesman during the Great Depression who believes fervently in the American Dream and the romantic fantasies of popular music. But his dreams of starting his own business are thwarted for lack of capital, and his wife Joan (Jessica Harper), who refuses to give him the inheritance money that she is saving – appropriately, given the film's title – for "a rainy day," is indifferent to passion, whether for entrepreneurship or for sex. (Harper, as discussed in the previous chapter, also starred in *Phantom of the Paradise* [1974].) On one of his regular sales trips, Arthur falls for and seduces a prim, repressed schoolteacher, Eileen. Immediately upon first seeing Eileen in a music shop, he is attracted to her and lip-syncs the song "Did You Ever See a Dream Walking?" with Bing Crosby's voice (Plate 33). In his musical fantasy Eileen is a more ethereal version of herself, irradiated by halo lighting and no longer stiff in her movements but through editing seeming to float to different spots around the store. Arthur desires Eileen physically

PLATE 33 *Pennies from Heaven*: Arthur (Steve Martin) kisses the vision of Eileen (Bernadette Peters) he imagines as "a dream walking" (Herbert Ross, 1981; Producers: Nora Kaye, Herbert Ross).

but salves his guilt by imagining her as a lady above reproach. Thus he becomes violently indignant when the store-owner makes a sexual remark about her, and again later when two fellow salesmen interpret his "love" as lust and assume Arthur has done the sexual things with her that he in fact does want to do. Unable to accept his own "animal" desires, as Joan would have it, Arthur masks them with the myths of popular music. "Birds do it, bees do it," Arthur pleads to Joan, filtering his desire for sex as "falling in love," as much for his benefit as for hers.

Eileen, who is seduced and then abandoned by Arthur, becomes pregnant, loses her job, leaves home, has an abortion, and turns to prostitution in order to survive. Arthur, who has returned home, manages to secure his wife's savings to open a record shop, but the business fails. Arthur meets Eileen again, by chance, as she is working the street, and they impulsively decide to abandon their lives and renew their relationship. At the same time, a blind girl (Elisha Krupka) is raped and killed by a vagrant hitchhiker identified in the credits as the Accordion Man (Vernel Bagneris), to whom Arthur had given a ride earlier in the film. Circumstantial evidence causes Arthur to be arrested, convicted, and sentenced to death for the murder of the girl. In the ending, Arthur is led to the gallows while Eileen waits at the window of a dingy hotel room. About to be hanged, he recites and then breaks into singing the lyrics of the title song – the only time in the film that he (or anyone else) actually sings a song (although, of course, it was post-synced in standard fashion).

Suddenly and inexplicably, Arthur and Ellen are together in a vague, almost abstract space, which is then brightly illuminated to reveal a large chorus which celebrates "The Glory of Love" with the happily reunited couple (Plate 34). This is Arthur's final (dying?) fantasy, one determined by his still unshakeable belief in the romantic vision of the pop songs he had sold. As Arthur says to Eileen when she asks how he got here, "We've worked too hard not to have a happy ending." Then, in the film's last, presumably ironic, shot, the camera reverses the movement of the opening shot as it climbs through rain and gathering clouds to a bright blue sky, where it leaves us with the same impossibly sunny positivism that Arthur has steadfastly embraced even to his sad and unjust end.

As already suggested, Martin's comic persona serves a purpose here, because ultimately the joke is on Arthur. Ironically, Arthur, a salesman, has himself been "sold" on the sunny ideology of popular music – the impossibly optimistic view that every cloud has a silver lining and that every time it rains, it rains pennies from heaven. Embracing, like the song, a staunchly upbeat perspective, Arthur's imagination transforms the blind girl into a mysterious beauty and the Accordion Man from a deferential

PLATE 34 *Pennies from Heaven*: Arthur's final utopian fantasy celebrates "The Glory of Love" as he is about to be executed.

stutterer (and, as we learn later, a sexual predator) into an eloquently expressive dancer, his posture of cloying subservience turning to the remarkable fluidity of a free, self-assured spirit as he dances the title number. When the dance begins, the drab roadside café where the two men are eating opens up like the Pullman Porter in the "Shuffle Off to Buffalo" number in *42nd Street* (1933), but only Arthur seems to notice. Earlier, when the bank manager refuses Arthur a loan to start his business because he has no collateral, suddenly the musical sequence "Yes, Yes (My Baby Said Yes, Yes Instead of No, No)" begins. The song's insistent positivism comes from Arthur's refusal to accept his actual rejection for a loan by the banker, and the choreography includes the two of them happily dancing together along with a line of tellers cheerfully bestowing sacks of money upon the salesman. At the end of the sequence, however, we see Arthur in his car, riding home dejectedly after being denied the loan.

Just as the diner pulls apart during the Accordion Man's dance to reveal something unperceived by others, so as in earlier musicals the other musical numbers in the film metaphorically pry open the characters who sing them to reveal their inner wishes and desires. However, while in earlier musicals singing and dancing tends to express love and joy, the desires of the characters in *Pennies from Heaven* are baser. As Pauline Kael noted in her review of the film, "It's a stylized mythology of the Depression which uses the popular songs of the period as expressions of people's deepest longings – for sex, for romance, for money, for a high good time" (Kael, 1984: 272). Thus, once Eileen's emotions have been stirred by meeting Arthur, she reimagines herself during a dull lesson in her classroom as a torch singer clad in a provocatively tight silver gown, lip-syncing and dancing the rollicking "Love Is Good for Anything That Ails You," accompanied by a swing band composed of her young students (Plate 35). The youngsters are suddenly dressed in matching white outfits and playing white pianos that have replaced their desks, an allusion to the chorus line with white pianos in Busby Berkeley's "The Words Are in My Heart" number from his *Gold Diggers of 1935* (1935). Later, Tom (Christopher Walken), a slick city operator, seduces a down-and-out Eileen with a tap dance/striptease routine on top of a bar while lip-syncing Cole Porter's "Let's Misbehave," which Eileen knows she will have to do in return for money. Similarly, Joan sings "It's a Sin to Tell a Lie" in response to her cheating husband, imagining stabbing him in the back with a pair of scissors and adding a layer of ominousness to Dolly Dawn's original vocal in the process.

Toward the end of the film, Arthur and Eileen go to the cinema, where they watch Astaire and Rogers in *Follow the Fleet* (1936). Arthur becomes

PLATE 35 *Pennies from Heaven*: Eileen imagines herself as a torch singer leading a swing band of her students playing "Love Is Good for Anything That Ails You."

transfixed by the film couple's romantic allure, he looking in awe at the screen as she watches him. Then Arthur and Eileen appear on the stage beneath the screen, dancing in perfect harmony with the towering images of Astaire and Rogers in the "Let's Face the Music and Dance" number. The larger images of Fred and Ginger, dwarfing Arthur and Eileen, at once suggest the mythic power of the former and the relative powerlessness of the latter. Indeed, the lyrics of the song ("facing the music") take on a more ominous undertone for Arthur, who shortly is to be arrested and wrongly convicted for a murder he did not commit. Then, suddenly, Arthur and Eileen are "in" the film within the film, dressed as Fred and Ginger, in a marvellous reconstruction of the original scene that suggests the way we project ourselves into the fantasy worlds of movies and, as Arthur does, of popular song.

Arthur insists that "songs tell the truth," but life as envisioned in *Pennies from Heaven* is hardly the romantic fantasy offered by the Astaire–Rogers musicals. A billboard advertising a movie entitled *Love before Breakfast* looms in the background by the bridge where several fateful events take place in the story for Arthur, who tries unsuccessfully to coax Joan into making love upon awakening in the morning in the film's first narrative scene. The disjunction between Arthur's imagination and the real world shows how torn he is between his own "animal" desire and the romantic visions of popular song. Not knowing how to distinguish his fantasy from reality regarding Eileen, Arthur is in a way as blind as the blind girl he meets, tellingly, in a tunnel, a metaphor for the narrowness of his worldview. It is no coincidence that the canes of the chorus line in his re-creation of "Let's Face the Music and Dance" seem to "grow" at the end of the number, filling the frame like prison bars and entrapping him.

In postmodern fashion, the film's production numbers pastiche numerous other musicals, a few of which have already been noted. In addition to its musical references, the film also re-creates as *tableaux vivants* four paintings, two by Reginald Marsh and two by Edward Hopper, including the iconic *Nighthawks* (1942) – all of which actually depict scenes of New York, not Chicago, but are associated with the "look" of the 1930s in popular memory. Thematically, the postmodern style of *Pennies from Heaven* is perfectly appropriate, for the film is about the tragic fate of a man who clings to the myths promulgated by popular music, who refuses to understand them with a postmodern awareness as ideological constructions. In that final shot, when the camera ascends from Arthur's fantasy through the storm clouds to reveal a now brilliant blue sky, the kind of vibrant sky that might be found in a Freed Unit Technicolor musical, a rainbow is momentarily visible. But in the world of *Pennies from Heaven*, that wonderful place somewhere over the rainbow occurs only in Arthur's imagination at the moment of his death. Meanwhile, the film's unconventional staging of its musical numbers distances viewers from Arthur even as we sympathize with his romantic dreams, thus preventing us from escaping into the musical's typically appealing utopian fantasies like Arthur, the model cultural dupe.

Quite unlike *Pennies from Heaven*, *Across the Universe*, a pastiche of the '60s counter-culture, views popular music – specifically, the music of The Beatles – as accurately expressing, reflecting, and influencing personal and social history. Incorporating thirty-two tunes written by members of The Beatles (John Lennon, Paul McCartney, George Harrison, and Ringo Starr) between 1962 and 1969, *Across the Universe* attempts to provide a cultural overview of the 1960s through the music of this one influential band. The film was directed by Julie Taymor (who also co-wrote the story), a theater and opera director who had made the transition to film with *Titus* (1999), a visually striking version of Shakespeare's *Titus Andronicus*, and *Frida* (2002), a biopic of Mexican artist Frida Kahlo starring Salma Hayek. For Taymor and her collaborators in *Across the*

Universe, the music of The Beatles represents myth not as illusion, as false ideology, but in the sense of embodying the cultural values of the time.

The film is a dense pastiche of counter-cultural lore, including but hardly limited to references to Timothy Leary, Ken Kesey, the Merry Pranksters, Jimi Hendrix, and Janis Joplin – sometimes in such forced and shallow ways that they seem to trivialize them. And, too, some of The Beatles references in the film are, admittedly, facile, such as the shipyard paymaster's comment that when he was younger he had thought he'd be long gone from there when he was 64 (a reference to "When I'm 64"); the remark made by Jude (Jim Sturgess) that Prudence (T.V. Carpio) had come into his apartment through the bathroom window ("She Came in through the Bathroom Window"); and Sadie (Dana Fuchs), named for the song "Sexy Sadie," telling Max (Joe Anderson) that although he looks clean-cut he might have murdered his grandmother with a hammer ("Maxwell's Silver Hammer"). (Like other characters in the film, Jude and Prudence are, of course, also named after Beatles songs – "Hey Jude" and "Dear Prudence," respectively.) But despite these moments, which threaten to turn the film into merely a game of spotting the reference, the reliance on The Beatles' music as a lens through which to view the history of their times works because, as Greil Marcus has written, The Beatles "became one with the times, merging with them rather than standing above them" (Marcus, 1976: 188). Also, there are inherent tensions in the music of The Beatles that reflect the social tensions that marked the decade of their popularity. If the 1960s was characterized by tensions between peaceful aspirations and violent realities, so in the music of Lennon and McCartney, as Marcus notes, there was a simultaneous pull between lyrical sensitivity and the insistence of the beat, with "John's songs describ[ing] struggle, while Paul's denied it" (Marcus, 1976: 187–8).

As the film begins, we see a young man, Jude, alone on a beach. As the camera tracks in to a close-up of his face, he sings the beginning of "Girl," which starts by asking "Is there anybody going to listen to my story/All about the girl who came to stay?" The girl, as we soon discover, is Lucy Carrigan (Evan Rachel Wood), a high school senior in Dayton, Ohio. But the story, as we also learn, is about a lot more than a boy-meets-girl, boy-loses-girl romance, as the image of Jude's face dissolves into shots of waves breaking furiously upon a shore, a metaphor for the social and political turbulence of the decade.

The metaphor then becomes explicit in further shots superimposed on the waves evoking the decade's civil rights demonstrations, the infamous killing of students during an anti-war protest at Kent State University (in Ohio, Lucy's home state) on May 4, 1970 by the Ohio National Guard (an event alluded to in Neil Young's "Ohio"), and soldiers fighting in Vietnam. This montage is accompanied by a verse of "Helter Skelter" (sung by Sadie, a Janis-Joplin like vocalist who appears later in the film), the title of which was originally a reference to an amusement park ride but was interpreted by cult leader Charles Manson to be about an impending apocalyptic racial war. The words were scrawled on a wall with their victims' blood by the Manson family after killing Sharon Tate and her friends in August 1969 (see Bugliosi and Gentry, 2001 [1974]). The choice of song here, in addition to the images, makes clear the film's view of the 1960s as a time marked by social tension and violence.

The title credit appears as the scene shifts to a high school dance in Dayton. The band is playing "Hold Me Tight," an early Beatles romantic tune in the manner of '50s pop rock. As the song plays, the scene cuts back and forth between the dance in Dayton and a club in Liverpool, England, where a band that looks similar to the early Beatles is also playing the song in a venue that resembles the Cavern, the Liverpool club where The Beatles started, where Jude is on a date with his girlfriend, Molly (Lisa Hogg). The dreariness of working-class Liverpool is visually contrasted to the wealth and luxury of suburban Dayton, a difference evoked later in the first conversation between Lucy and Jude, when she refers to braces as orthodontic devices for straightening teeth and he as a device for keeping your trousers up. Despite the class differences of the film's romantic couple, however, like everyone else they will be caught up in the unfolding events of the decade. Eventually Lucy will come east and meet Jude in New York City, a narrative structure that recalls Milos Forman's film version of "the hippie musical" *Hair* (1979), in which a straight Midwestern youth (John Savage) comes to New York, where by happenstance he meets and becomes involved with the hippie Berger (Treat Williams). The reference here is hardly arbitrary, as both films feature free-spirited main characters – Berger in *Hair*, Lucy's brother Max in *Across the Universe* – who are swallowed up by the military and sent to Vietnam.

Both Jude's and Lucy's relationships are experiencing the tensions of impending change: Lucy's boyfriend Daniel (Spencer Liff) is about to be inducted into the Army to fight in Vietnam, while Jude, a shipyard worker, has joined the Merchant Navy and is going to ship out to the United States, where he plans to jump ship and find his father, a former GI who had a brief wartime affair with his mother and whom he has never met. As Jude ships out and Molly bids him goodbye, he sings "All My Lovin'," in which he promises to "write home every day." Now the film intercuts a scene featuring Lucy kissing Daniel farewell as he leaves for basic training, after which we see her writing him a letter and him reading it while in a troop transport. Soon, however, the writing will stop as Daniel will be killed in Vietnam and Jude will fall for Lucy, forgetting Molly, who in turn will end up pregnant and in a rebound relationship with another shipyard worker.

A shot of a tractor ploughing a field while a caravan of Army troop trucks travels in the opposite direction on the nearby road graphically hints at the social changes that are already in motion and that will eventually sweep up the film's characters. The Army trucks pass the high school football field where the team is practicing, and one of the cheerleaders, Prudence, sings "I Wanna Hold Your Hand." As she sings, she glances at one of the other cheerleaders talking to one of the players, whom we see together in a two-shot. The viewer is likely to assume that the object of her secret affection is the player, but he soon leaves the frame and it becomes clear that the object of Prudence's desire is in fact the cheerleader. At this early point in the decade, her gay desire is privately expressed in the song but not revealed publicly. Yet the song's lyrics again hint at the social revolution already brewing: "It's such a feeling that my love I can't hide," Prudence sings, anticipating the emphatic rise of the gay liberation movement that would begin at the end of the decade with the Stonewall Uprising in June 1969. Interestingly, Prudence sings these lyrics as she walks through a cluster of macho football players tackling each other in slow motion, which turns what might seem like merely the sport's violent contact into a series of possible homoerotic embraces.

Jude hitchhikes to Princeton, New Jersey, in search of his father (Robert Clohessy), who turns out to be a janitor rather than the professor he had imagined. Jude's coming to America suggests the "British Invasion," the wave of British pop music, spearheaded by The Beatles and The Rolling Stones, which would wash across the United States in the 1960s and change American popular music irrevocably. His paternal search parallels the British rock bands' embrace of the roots of rock 'n' roll in the blues and rhythm 'n' blues music of poor black Americans, a parallel reinforced by Jude's father's blue-collar job and basement apartment, where he lives in the foundation of Princeton's cultural edifices.

While at Princeton, Jude becomes friends with Max, a rebellious student. After they meet, Max sings "With a Little Help from My Friends" as they drink and smoke pot with some of his college mates, cavorting about the campus like The Beatles in Richard Lester's *A Hard Day's Night* (1964). Similarly upbeat, Lucy receives a telegram from Daniel that he will be coming home on leave, and her joyous anticipation is accompanied by her singing "It Won't Be Long" ("You're coming home, yeah, yeah ... every day we'll be happy I know"). As she sings the song, ecstatic in gym and even in math class, the song carries over a shot of Max coming home for Thanksgiving with Jude, who will be captivated by Lucy immediately upon meeting her, thus anticipating the eventual relationship that will develop between them. When the three go bowling together after Thanksgiving dinner, Jude sings "I've Just Seen a Face," his blossoming romantic feelings expressed by the suddenly rhythmic choreography of the bowlers. And when he sings the line, "Falling, yes I am falling, and she keeps calling me back again," we see a shot from above of Jude, so bowled over by Lucy that he seems to slide down the bowling lane as if it were now upright like a chute instead of laying on the ground.

Max drops out of Princeton, and he and Jude move to New York City, where they rent rooms in the Greenwich Village apartment of sexy singer Sadie. They are excited about being in the Big Apple and the potential pleasures the city offers, but when they look out the window they are just two more New Yorkers in a little window surrounded by a vast brick wall. The image not only recalls the dreary brick rowhouses of Liverpool, but also suggests their entrapment by the winds of change stirred by larger social forces represented by the large and impersonal city. At the same time as two soldiers deliver the news of Daniel's death in action, a race riot explodes in Detroit. Trapped in the riot's violence, a young black boy (Timmy Mitchum) cowers by an overturned, burnt-out car in the street singing "Let it Be," its peaceful message clearly unheeded by the looters and the National Guardsmen who are shooting them (Plate 36). The song is taken over by a chorus of gospel singers as the images intercut Daniel's burial in Arlington National Cemetary and the funeral of the black boy, two victims of the era's political violence.

The dead boy's older brother, the guitarist Jo-Jo (Martin Luther McCoy), named for a character in The Beatles' "Get Back" and associated in a number of ways with Jimi Hendrix, arrives in New York City to the tune of "Come Together." The first verse of the song is sung by a bum in the Port Authority bus station, then picked up by a pimp along with prostitutes in the streets, and then by an aging hippie (all three roles played by singer Joe Cocker), with a choreographed dance by a street full of business executives in suits with briefcases. (Cocker, as we saw in Chapter 7, is associated with The Beatles through his Woodstock performance of "With a Little Help from My Friends.") The song not only expresses the period's fleeting hope for social unity but also refers to the turns of the plot at this point, as the film's major characters all cross paths: Jo-Jo, after being almost run over by Max, who is now driving taxi for a living, successfully auditions for Sadie's band, The Po Boys; Prudence then comes in through Jude and Max's apartment's bathroom window after being beaten by an

PLATE 36 *Across the Universe*: Jo-Jo's brother (Timmy Mitchum), trapped in an inner-city race riot, sings part of The Beatles' "Let it Be" (Julie Taymor, 2007; Producers: Matthew Gross, Jennifer Todd, Suzanne Todd). Courtesy of Photofest.

abusive boyfriend. The circle is completed when Lucy decides to visit her brother Max to deliver his Army induction notice, despite her mother's small-town fear that she'll be corrupted in the imposing metropolis. "The big bad city's not going to get me," Lucy reassures her mother, adding that "I don't even smoke"; but a sudden cut to Sadie and her band on a New York stage performing "Why Don't We Do It in the Road," with Lucy along with her brother, Jude, and Prudence in the audience, foreshadows the era's counter-cultural politics of sexual liberation ("No one will be watching us/Why don't we do it in the road?") and flaunts the decadence that her mother fears.

In perhaps the most inventively staged number in the film, Max, having received his notice from Lucy, shows up at the Army Induction Center for his physical exam. "I Want You (She's So Heavy)" begins with posters of Uncle Sam (with the familiar phrase "Uncle Sam Wants You") suddenly becoming animate. Uncle Sam's arms reach out from the poster, grab Max by the shoulders, and shove him in into a hallway lined on both sides with soldiers with identical, impossibly angular faces. Their harsh countenances, with jaws so square they seem to express monstrousness rather than steadfastness or determination, effectively express Max's view of the Army as institutionalized collective violence. Max is moved through the gauntlet of soldiers on a conveyor belt, suggesting the Army as consuming a generation of young American men as grist for its military machine. He is stripped to his underwear and moved to another room with many other boys similarly undressed, where a platoon of the hard-faced soldiers perform a peculiar choreography, as much military drill as dance, with crisply angular, somewhat threatening movements of their arms and legs as they sing "I want you, I want you so bad." The inductees are thrust into a series of metal boxes that emphasize their entrapment and scrutiny by the "Establishment." (They are "inspected, detected, infected, neglected, and selected," in the words of Arlo Guthrie's anti-war anthem "Alice's Restaurant," made into a film of the same name by Arthur Penn in 1969.) As The Beatles' song shifts to the lyrics "she's so heavy," the young men, still in their underwear, trudge through a miniature jungle carrying a replica of the Statue of Liberty – a graphic depiction of the burden of freedom borne by America's young men at the time, part of the official rhetoric in support of the war in Vietnam.

The number ends with Max wrapped in plastic and classified "A1," a made-in-USA product ready to be shipped to Southeast Asia for combat, while Sadie and Jo-Jo, who have fallen for each other, dance closely as Prudence looks on from outside, singing the final "I want you so bad" to express her now unrequited yearning for Sadie. The lovelorn Prudence locks herself in her room, but is coaxed out by the others to the tune of – what else? – "Dear Prudence." As they sing the injunction to "open up your eyes, look around," their apartment changes into a Magritte-like blue sky, and while the song continues, Prudence rejoins the world as it concludes with all of them now marching in an anti-war protest in Washington Square. But this clearly joyful solidarity, as in *Woodstock* (1970, see Chapter 7), soon splinters, anticipating the imminent dissolution of the decade's idealism. At a launch party for the new book by the Timothy Leary-like guru Dr Robert (Bono), named for another Beatles' tune not sung in the film, Jude, Lucy, Max, and Jo-Jo drink punch laced with LSD. The images become saturated with psychedelic colors as Dr Robert sings "I Am the Walrus" with its surreal lyrics ("elementary penguin singing Hare Krishna/Man, you should have seen them kicking Edgar Allan Poe").

As the song continues, the stoned foursome literally go far out, joining Dr Robert on his "Beyond" psychedelic bus tour across America and then finding themselves deposited somewhere at the site of a strange circus. Here, the ringmaster, Mr Kite (Eddie Izzard), sings "For the Benefit of Mr Kite" accompanied by bizarre creatures resembling the Blue Meanies from The Beatles' animated film *Yellow Submarine* (1968) (Plate 37). Animation and special effects make Mr Kite's circus appear psychedelic, all of it taking place in an impossibly small tent, suggesting the expanded consciousness that so many were seeking at the time through drugs. Following this, the group wander into a field singing "Because," with its appropriate lyrics of stoned wonder ("Because the world is round it turns me on"). They lay in a circular pattern in the tall grass, their geometric arrangement expressing their oneness with nature, the camera pulling up and away as they sing "Because the wind is high it blows my mind." If the Detroit riots represented the "long, hot summer" of 1967, these scenes with Dr Robert and Mr Kite invoke the summer of love that same year, when hippie congregations in major cities across North America gained the attention of the national media along with the conflagrations of inner city riots.

The shot dissolves into another, of the characters swimming underwater, embracing each other in slow motion, as if a celebration of pure polymorphous pleasure. But as Max swims, the shadow of a helicopter engulfs him and there is a sudden cut to him in combat in the jungles of Vietnam. Meanwhile, Sadie decides to leave The Po Boys, and in their final public gig together, Jo-Jo sabotages the performance by playing discordant notes and interrupting Sadie's singing with his own. Ironically,

PLATE 37 *Across the Universe*: Mr Kite (Eddie Izzard) sings the benefits of his psychedelic circus. Courtesy of Photofest.

as the couple, as well as the band, are now in the throes of splitting up, the song they are performing is "Oh, Darling!," with lyrics in which the singer begs their partner not to leave because "I can't make it alone." At the same time, Lucy becomes increasingly involved in the anti-war movement while Jude grows jealous of the time she spends with Paco (Logan Marshall-Green), one of the protest leaders. More apolitical and involved in his art, Jude withdraws from the televised news coverage of fighting in Vietnam into a marijuana haze as he sings "Strawberry Fields Forever."

In the song, though, Jude comes to the realization that "living is easy with eyes closed, misunderstanding all you see"; and, so inspired, he begins to use strawberries in his art, an image that later becomes the logo for Sadie's record label, an allusion to The Beatles' Apple Records. But in the film the strawberry serves as much more than an oblique reference to The Beatles' unfortunate business enterprise. Indeed, it represents the tension or duality that informs both The Beatles' music and the film's vision of the 1960s, at once representing natural beauty and bounty (think, for example, of Ingmar Bergman's *Wild Strawberries* [1957]) and the blood being spilled both at home in domestic dissent and overseas in Vietnam. In the montage accompanying the song as it moves from Jude singing it alone in his room to Max singing it as he engages in a firefight – in other words, from the utopia of strawberry fields to the nightmarish killing fields of Vietnam – we see strawberries dripping luscious red juice, and when they dissolve into grenades the juice seems more like blood oozing from open wounds.

As the film reaches its dramatic climax, Jude's singing of the gentle ballad "Across the Universe" overlaps with a reprise of Sadie performing "Helter Skelter" to a montage of a violent demonstration at Columbia University, where both Lucy and Jude, now separated, are arrested. We see Jude being beaten by police, blood running down his face like strawberry juice, the scene crosscut with Max in a battle in Vietnam. Max returns home wounded and addicted to morphine, singing "Happiness is a Warm Gun" in the VA hospital ("I need a fix 'cause I'm going down"), while Jude is deported back to England, returning us to the narrative point where the film began, with Jude sitting by the ocean thinking of Lucy. On the sound track, "A Day in the Life" reaches its famous final elongated, torturous note, here performed as non-diegetic music by guitarist Jeff Beck, as both Jude in Liverpool and Max in New York sit in bars drinking beer and feeling sorry for themselves.

However, at this seeming nadir for the two men, the film asserts its own unambiguously positive message. Max begins to sing "Hey Jude," with its advice to "take a sad song and make it better," which is exactly what Jude does as he decides to return legally to the United States and possibly reconnect with Lucy. As he leaves home for the journey, the sun suddenly breaks through the dreary Liverpool sky and all the children playing in the street follow him, joining in the chorus of the song, the world seeming to be in tune with his renewed feelings of hope and love. Arriving in New York, Jude is met by Max, who takes him in his taxi to Sadie's free rooftop concert – a reference to The Beatles' final, impromptu performance on the roof of Apple Records in downtown London in January 1969 – where she has apparently reunited with Jo-Jo and they are singing "Don't Let Me Down." "I'm in love for the first time, and you know it's gonna last," Sadie and Jo-Jo sing, as much to each other as to the crowd.

The police arrive to break up the concert, and after the crowd disperses, Jude, alone on the roof, goes up to one of the microphones, still on, and sings "All You Need is Love." In contrast to their earlier violence in the film (and to the actual Beatles event), the police relent – "nothing you can do that can't be done," as the song triumphantly declares – and Sadie and her band "come together" on the roof once more to join in the song (Plate 38). As a result, Lucy hears the message and Jude spots Lucy on a rooftop across the street as the band begins the

PLATE 38 *Across the Universe*: Jude (Jim Sturgess, right) delivers the final message that "All You Need is Love," accompanied (left) by Jo-Jo (Martin Luther McCoy) and Sadie (Dana Fuchs) and (back) by Max (Joe Anderson) and Prudence (T.V. Carpio). Courtesy of Photofest.

refrain "Love is all you need." Jude's musical message spans the literal gulf between them, and the final image before the credits is a close-up of Lucy's face, returning the loving gaze of Jude, a brilliant blue sky behind her as the chorus chants "She loves you, yeah, yeah, yeah."

This upbeat ending, despite the social upheaval that had preceded it, insists that love can carry across space and time ("across the universe"). It might seem as if this ending lacks real conviction after all that has come before, and certainly it flies in the face of history, which has hardly grown less violent, since the end of the 1960s. For many viewers, *Across the Universe* ends on a sentimental, if not saccharine, endorsement of "love," whether in personal or public politics – the very thing that brings about the demise of poor Arthur Parker in *Pennies from Heaven*. Yet in so doing, *Across the Universe*, despite its many differences from the earliest film musicals and the changes in popular music and listener taste, brings us back once again to the romantic and utopian thrust at the heart of the genre.

REFERENCES

Altman, Rick 1987. *The American Film Musical*. Bloomington: Indiana University Press.

Babington, Bruce, and William Peter Evans 1985. *Blue Skies and Silver Linings: Aspects of the Hollywood Musical*. Manchester and Dover, NH: Manchester University Press.

Barthes, Roland 1972. *Mythologies*, ed. and trans. Annette Lavers. New York: Hill and Wang.

Barthes, Roland 1977. "The Grain of the Voice." In *Image–Music–Text*, ed. and trans. Stephen Heath, pp. 179–89. New York: Hill and Wang.

Bartholomew, David 1975. "De Palma of the Paradise." *Cinefantastique* 4, no. 2 (Summer): 8–14.

Bennett, Andy 2004. "Everybody's Happy, Everybody's Free: Representation and Nostalgia in the Woodstock Film." In *Remembering Woodstock*, ed. Andy Bennett, pp. 43–54. Burlington, VT: Ashgate.

Berg, Charles M. 1978. "Cinema Sings the Blues." *Cinema Journal* 17, no. 2 (Spring): 1–12.

Biskind, Peter 1998. *Easy Riders, Raging Bulls*. New York: Simon & Schuster.

Bliss, Michael 1983. *Brian De Palma*. Metuchen, NJ: Scarecrow Press.

Bordwell, David, Janet Staiger, and Kristin Thompson 1985. *The Classical Hollywood Cinema: Film Style and Mode of Production to 1960*. New York: Columbia University Press.

Bourget, Jean-Loup 2003. "Social Implications in the Hollywood Genres." In *Film Genre Reader III*, ed. Barry Keith Grant, pp. 51–9. Austin: University of Texas Press.

Braudy, Leo 1977. *The World in a Frame: What We See in Films*. Garden City, NY: Anchor Doubleday.

Bugliosi, Vincent, and Curt Gentry 2001 [1974]. *Helter Skelter: The True Story of the Manson Murders*. New York: Norton.

Burns, Gary 1988. "Film and Popular Music." In *Film and the Arts in Symbiosis: A Resource Guide*, ed. Gary R. Edgerton, pp. 217–42. New York: Greenwood Press.

Cawelti, John 2003. "*Chinatown* and Generic Transformation in Recent American Films." In *Film Genre Reader III*, ed. Barry Keith Grant, pp. 243–61. Austin: University of California Press.

Charters, Samuel 1970. *The Poetry of the Blues*. New York: Avon.

Cohan, Steven 1993. "'Feminizing' the Song-and-Dance Man: Fred Astaire and the Spectacle of Masculinity in the Hollywood Musical." In *Screening the Male: Exploring Masculinities in Hollywood Cinema*, ed. Steven Cohan and Ina Rae Hark, pp. 46–69. London and New York: Routledge.

Cohn, Nik 1976. "Tribal Rites of the New Saturday Night," *New York* magazine, June. *http://nymag.com/nightlife/features/45933/*, accessed November 11, 2011.

Coursodon, Jean-Pierre, with Pierre Sauvage 1983. *American Directors*, vol. II. New York: McGraw-Hill, 1983.

Croce, Arlene 1972. *The Fred Astaire and Ginger Rogers Book*. New York: Vintage Books.

Doherty, Thomas 1988. *Teenagers and Teenpics: The Juvenilization of American Movies in the 1950s*. Boston: Unwin Hyman.

Dowdy, Andrew 1975. *The Films of the Fifties*. New York: Morrow.

Dyer, Richard 1980. "Entertainment and Utopia." In *Genre: The Musical*, ed. Rick Altman, pp. 175–89. London: Routledge and Kegan Paul.

Dyer, Richard 1990. "In Defense of Disco." In *On Record: Rock, Pop, and the Written Word*, ed. Simon Frith and Andrew Goodwin, pp. 410–18. New York: Pantheon.

Ebert, Roger. "Ebert's Glossary of Movie Terms." *http://academic.sun.ac.za/forlang/bergman/tech/glossary/ebert_glos.htm*, accessed October 26, 2011.

Ehrenstein, David, and Bill Reed 1982. *Rock on Film*. New York: Delilah Books.

Eisenberg, Evan 1987. *The Recording Angel: The Experience of Music from Aristotle to Zappa*. New York: Penguin.

Eisenstein, Sergei 1949. "Through Theater to Cinema." In *Film Form: Essays in Film Theory*, ed. Jay Leyda, pp. 3–17. New York: Harcourt, Brace & World.

Elsaesser, Thomas 1981. "Vincente Minnelli" (1970). In *Genre: The Musical*, ed. Rick Altman, pp. 8–27. London: Routledge and Kegan Paul.

Feuer, Jane 1993. *The Hollywood Musical*. 2nd edn. Bloomington: Indiana University Press.

Fischer, Lucy 1980. "The Image of Woman as Image: The Optical Politics of *Dames*." In *Genre: The Musical*, ed. Rick Altman, pp. 70–84. London: Routledge and Kegan Paul.

Fordin, Hugh 1975. *The World of Entertainment: Hollywood's Greatest Musicals*. New York: Avon.

Frith, Simon 1987. "Towards an Aesthetic of Popular Music." In *Music and Society*, ed. Susan McClary and Richard Leppart, pp. 133–49. Cambridge and New York: Cambridge University Press.

Frith, Simon, and Angela McRobbie 1990. "Rock and Sexuality." In *On Record: Rock, Pop and the Written Word*, ed. Simon Frith and Andrew Goodwin, pp. 371–89. New York: Pantheon.

Fuller, Richard 1972. "'Survive, Survive, Survive': Frederick Wiseman's New Documentary: *Basic Training*." *The Film Journal* 1, nos 3–4 (Fall–Winter): 74–9.

Furia, Philip, and Laurie Patterson 2010. *The Songs of Hollywood*. New York: Oxford University Press.

Gabbard, Krin 1996. *Jammin' at the Margins: Jazz and the American Cinema*. Chicago: University of Chicago Press.

Godard, Jean-Luc 1972. *Godard on Godard*, ed. Jean Narboni and Tom Milne. New York: Viking Press.

Goldstein, Richard 1969. *The Poetry of Rock*. New York: Bantam.

Gomez, Joseph 1976. *Ken Russell*. London: Frederick Muller.

Gourse, Leslie 1984. *Louis' Children: American Jazz Singers*. New York: Morrow.

Grant, Barry Keith 1986. "The Classic Hollywood Musical and the 'Problem' of Rock 'n' Roll." *Journal of Popular Film and Television* 13, no. 4 (Winter): 195–205.

Green, Lucy 1988. *Music on Deaf Ears: Musical Meaning, Ideology, Education*. Manchester: Manchester University Press/New York: St Martin's Press.

Hall, Sheldon, and Steve Neale 2010. *Epics, Spectacles, and Blockbusters*. Detroit: Wayne State University Press.

Hasbany, Richard 1978. "*Saturday Night Fever* and *Nashville*: Exploring the Comic Mythos." *Journal of Popular Culture* 12, no. 3 (Winter): 557–71.

Higham, Charles, and Joel Greenberg 1972. *The Celluloid Muse: Hollywood Directors Speak*. New York: New American Library.

Hillier, Jim, and Douglas Pye 2011. *100 Film Musicals*. London: British Film Institute/Palgrave Macmillan.

Hoberman, J. 1993. *42nd Street*. London: British Film Institute.

Johnson, Albert 1962. "*West Side Story*." *Film Quarterly* 15, no. 4 (Summer): 58–60.

Kael, Pauline 1964. *I Lost It at the Movies*. Boston: Little, Brown.

Kael, Pauline 1980. *When the Lights Go Down*. New York: Holt, Rinehart and Winston.

Kael, Pauline 1984. *Taking It All In*. New York: Holt, Rinehart and Winston.

Kantor, Bernard R., Irwin R. Blacker, and Anne Kramer 1970. *Directors at Work: Interviews with American Film-Makers*. New York: Funk & Wagnalls.

Kaplan, E. Ann 1987. *Rocking Around the Clock: Music Television, Postmodernism, and Consumer Culture*. New York and London: Routledge.

Kingman, David 1979. *American Music: A Panorama*. New York: Schirmer.

Knight, Arthur 2002. *Disintegrating the Musical: Black Performance and the American Musical Film*. Durham, NC: Duke University Press.

Kreuger, Miles, ed. 1975. *The Movie Musical from Vitaphone to 42nd Street, as Reported in a Great Fan Magazine*. New York: Dover.

McLuhan, Marshall 1964. *Understanding Movies: The Extensions of Man*. New York: Signet.

Marcus, Greil 1976. "The Beatles." In *The Rolling Stone Illustrated History of Rock & Roll*, ed. Jim Miller, pp. 177–89. New York: Random House/Rolling Stone Press.

Mast, Gerald 1987. *Can't Help Singin': The American Musical on Stage and Screen*. New York: Overlook Press.

Minnelli, Vincente, with Hector Arce 1974. *I Remember It Well*. New York: Berkley.

Moore, Allan F. 2004. "The Contradictory Aesthetics of Woodstock." In *Remembering Woodstock*, ed. Andy Bennett, pp. 75–89. Burlington, VT: Ashgate.

Mueller, John 1986. *Astaire Dancing: The Musical Films*. London: Hamish Hamilton.

Mulvey, Laura 1989. "Visual Pleasure and Narrative Cinema." In *Visual and Other Pleasures*, pp. 14–26. Bloomington: Indiana University Press.

Neale, Steve 1993. "Masculinity as Spectacle." In *Screening the Male: Exploring Masculinities in Hollywood Cinema*, ed. Steven Cohan and Ina Rae Hark, pp. 9–20. London and New York: Routledge.

Parkinson, David 2007. *The Rough Guide to Film Musicals*. London and New York: Rough Guides Ltd.

Pechter, William S. 1982. "Gray Skies, Scowling at Me." In *Movies Plus One: Seven Years of Film Reviewing*, pp. 73–86. New York: Horizon Press.

Polan, Dana 2009. "It Could Be Oedpius Rex: Denial and Difference in *The Band Wagon*; or, the American Musical as American Gothic." In *Vincente Minnelli: The Art of Entertainment*, ed. Joe McElhaney, pp. 130–53. Detroit: Wayne State University Press.

Prendergast, Roy M. 1987. *Film Music: A Neglected Art*. New York: Norton.

Rogin, Michael 1996. *Blackface, White Noise: Jewish Immigrants in the Hollywood Melting Pot*. Berkeley: University of California Press.

Rose, Lloyd 1982. "A Dreamer, Not a Storyteller." *Atlantic* (August): 88–92.

Roszak, Theodore 1969. *The Making of a Counter-Culture: Reflections on the Technocratic Society and Its Opposition*. Garden City, NY: Doubleday Anchor.

Roth, Mark 1980. "Some Warners Musicals and the Spirit of the New Deal." In *Genre: The Musical*, ed. Rick Altman, pp. 41–56. London: Routledge and Kegan Paul.

Sarris, Andrew 1968. *The American Cinema: Directors and Directions, 1929–1968*. New York: Dutton.

Schatz, Thomas 1981. *Hollywood Genres: Formula, Filmmaking, and the Studio System*. New York: Random House.

Shaw, Arnold 1982. *Dictionary of American Pop/Rock*. New York: Schirmer.

Siegel, Joel 1971. "*The Pirate*." *Film Heritage* 7, no. 1 (Fall): 21–32.

Smith, Susan 2005. *The Musical: Race, Gender and Performance*. London: Wallflower Press.

Stern, Lee Edward 1974. *The Movie Musical*. New York: Pyramid.

Thomas, Tony, and Jim Terry 1973. *The Busby Berkeley Book*. Greenwich, CT: New York Graphic Society.

Turner, Frederick Jackson 1961. "The Significance of the Frontier in American History" (1893), in *Frontier and Section: Selected Essays of Frederick Jackson Turner*, ed. Ray Allen Billington, pp. 37–62. Englewood Cliffs, NJ: Prentice-Hall.

Whiteley, Sheila 2004. "'1, 2, 3, What Are We Fighting 4': Music, Meaning and 'The Star-Spangled Banner.'" In *Remembering Woodstock*, ed. Andy Bennett, pp. 19–28. Burlington, VT: Ashgate.

Williams, Alan 1980. "Is Sound Recording Like a Language?" *Yale French Studies* no. 60 (1980): 51–66.

Wills, Nadine. 2001. "'100 Per Cent Woman': The Crotch Shot in the Hollywood Musical." *Screen* 42, no. 2 (Summer): 121–41.

Woll, Allen L. 1983. *The Hollywood Musical Goes to War*. Chicago: Nelson-Hall.

Wollen, Peter 1992. *Singin' in the Rain*. London: British Film Institute.

Wood, Michael 1975. *America in the Movies*. New York: Delta.

Wood, Robin 1979. "Never Never Change: Always Gonna Dance." *Film Comment* 15, no. 5 (September–October): 29–31.

Wood, Robin 2009. "Minnelli's *Madame Bovary*." In *Vincente Minnelli: The Art of Entertainment*, ed. Joe McElhaney, pp. 155–66. Detroit: Wayne State University Press.

Zappa, Frank 1970. "50s Teenagers and 50s Rock." *Evergreen* (August): 43–6.

INDEX

Boldface type indicates plates.

The Hollywood Film Musical, First Edition. Barry Keith Grant.
© 2012 Barry Keith Grant. Published 2012 by Blackwell Publishing Ltd.

Kelly, Gene, 3, 5, 20–4, **23**, 31, 33, 45, 46, 52, 85–98, **96**, **97**
Kenton, Stan, 30
Kern, Jerome, 10, 11, 16
Kesey, Ken, 154
Key, Francis Scott, 125
Kibbee, Guy, 56, **61**
Kidd, Michael, 20, 22
Killers, The (1946), 148
King Creole, 47
King of Jazz, The, 14, 27, 52–3
Kiss, 139, 141
Knight, Arthur, 53
Knight, Gladys, 37
Kopple, Barbara, 117
Kornfeld, Artie, 117, 129
Krause, Werner, 140
Kristofferson, Kris, 136
Kubrick, Stanley, 33, 109–10

LaBelle, Patti, 36
Lady Gaga, 139
Lamour, Dorothy, 24
Lancaster, Burt, 148
Lang, Mike, 118, 119, 126, 129
Lantz, Walter, 13–14
Last Waltz, The, 118
Laughton, Charles, 71
Laurel, Stan, 14
Leacock, Richard, 28
Leary, Timothy, 154
Lee, Alvin, 123
Lee, Ang, 118
Lee, Doris, 88
Lee, Spike, 9
Lelouch, Claude, 135
Lennon, John, 123, 154
Lenny, 35
Leroux, Gaston, 132
LeRoy, Mervyn, 57
Lester, Richard, 26, 156
Lévi-Strauss, Claude, 41
Lights of New York, The, 11
Lion King, The, 36

Lisztomania, 31
Little Caesar, 57
Little Johnny Jones, 10
Little Mermaid, The, 36
Little Nellie Kelly, 18
Little Prince, The, 26
Little Richard, 25, 51, 52
Little Shop of Horrors, 37, 53
Lloyd, Frank, 71
Lloyd Webber, Andrew, 132
Lonely Boy, 28–9
Love Me or Leave Me, 20
Love Me Tonight, 13
Love Parade, The, 2, 13
Loving You, 47–8
Loy, Myrna, 14
Lubitsch, Ernst, 2, 5, 13
Lucas, George, 1, 131
Luce, Clare Booth, 26
Luhrmann, Baz, 5, 35–6
Lymon, Frankie, 27

McCartney, Paul, 154
McCoy, Martin Luther, 157, **162**
McDonald, Country Joe, 123–4
MacDonald, Jeanette, 5, 13, 14
MacLaine, Shirley, 35, 146
McLuhan, Marshall, 9
MacMahon, Aline, 56
McRobbie, Angela, 142
Madame Bovary (1949), 86, 98
Madonna, 5, 36
Madonna: Truth or Dare, 29
Magnificent Ambersons, The, 100
Mahler, 31
mambo, 104–6
Mamet, David, 147
Mamma Mia!, 2
Mamoulian, Rouben, 13
Man and a Woman, A, 134
Manchurian Candidate, The (1962), 143
Mangeshkar, Lata, 5
Maniac, 30
Mann, Herbie, 109

Sweet Charity, 35
Sweet Rosie O'Grady, 19
swing music, 25–6, 30
Swing Time, 9, 17

Taking Woodstock, 118–19, 122
Tales of Hoffman, 5
Talmadge, Norma, 41
Tamblyn, Russ, 40
T.A.M.I. Show, The, 28
Tashlin, Frank, 25
Tate, Sharon, 155
Tavares, 112
Taylor, Dwight, 72
Taymor, Julie, 153, 10, 92
Teenage Caveman, 25
Teenage Monster, 25
television, 24, 37
Temple, Shirley, 5
Ten Years After, 122, 123
Thackeray, William Makepeace, 76
Thank God It's Friday, 108
That Night in Rio, 19
That's Entertainment, 22, 34
That's Entertainment II, 22, 34
They Met in Argentina, 19
This is Spinal Tap, 29
This is the Army, 19
Thomas, B.J., 31
Thousands Cheer, 22
Three Little Words, 20
Thriller (1983), 131
Thunderbolt, 55
Tiber, Elliott, 118
Till the Clouds Roll By, 11
Tin Pan Alley, 7, 10, 36, 122
Tin Pan Alley, 19
Titus, 153
Tommy, 31, **32**, 32–3
Top Hat, 16, 33, 43, 70–84, **75**, **80**, **82**, 91, 115
Touch of Evil, 139
Townsend, Pete, 120
Travolta, John, 108, 111, **113**

Trumbauer, Frankie, 52
Trumbo, Dalton, 123
Turner, Frederick Jackson, 55
Turner, Tina, 32
Turning Point, The, 146
Twentieth Century-Fox Records, 30
Twist Around the Clock, 27
2001: A Space Odyssey, 109

Umbrellas of Cherbourg, The, see: parapluies de Cherbourg, Les
Under the Roofs of Paris, see: Sous les toits de Paris
Underworld, 55
Universal Pictures, 30
Untouchables, The, 132

Vallee, Rudy, 147
Varèse, Edgar, 39
vaudeville, 7, 9, 10, 14
Vertigo, 132
vie est un roman, La [Life is a Bed of Roses], 5
Vincent, Gene, 25
Vitaphone, 11
von Sternberg, Josef, 55
von Tilzer, Harry, 9

Wadleigh, Michael, 117, 123–5, 129, 134
Wallace, Oliver, 18
Wand, Betty, 40
Warner, Jack, 64
Warner Bros, 11–12, 13, 14–16, 18, 20, 25, 30, 38, 45, 55–7, 64, 116–17, 136, 145
Warner Bros Records, 30
Warner Communications Inc. (WCI), 30
Warren, Harry, 15, 57, 71
Warren, William, 56
Weekend, 126
Weekend in Havana, 19
Weintraub, Fred, 116–17

2000

Mamma Mia 2008
 by Phyillida Lloyd

Newsies
   seize the day 1:40
   king of N Y.
   World will know.
   Once + for all.
   Santa Fe 1:28.

Most of cast traind + dance
+ martial Art 6 weeks before
filmg command

      1:30

Do No - Review G.B. project sheet Handout
    Decide by next class
      Discuss

1930's cont.
Most famous Dance Team #of films
                  B.B. lived
Intro Review Astaire

Intro Review Ginger

Intro. Top Hat - B.G.
      Director creates dolly.

Compare contrast to 42nd street.

Dance their way through the depression

1980
Annie
Fame ⊗
Pennies from Heaven
Popeye
Beat street
* Krush Groove* 1985 Michael Schultz
    Purple Rain 1984
Little shop of Horrors 1986
_____
1990's
Steppin Out 1991
The commitments
That thing you do Tom Hanks
Newsie Disney
  Cry Baby